The Ultimate Hot Chocolate Bombs Cookbook

100 Delicious Recipes for Homemade Chocolate Spheres to Satisfy Your Sweet Tooth

Sharon Wood

Copyright Material ©2023

All Rights Reserved

No part of this book may be used or transmitted in any form or by any means without the proper written consent of the publisher and copyright owner, except for brief quotations used in a review. This book should not be considered a substitute for medical, legal, or other professional advice.

TABLE OF CONTENTS

TABLE OF CONTENTS 3
INTRODUCTION..7
   1. Matcha Hot chocolate bombs 8
   2. Cotton Candy Chocolate Bombs 10
   3. Pumpkin Spice Hot Chocolate Bombs................. 12
   4. Hot Chocolate Bombs 14
   5. Rainbow White Hot Chocolate Bombs 16
   6. Marble Chocolate Egg.. 18
   7. Rum Chata Hot Cocoa Bombs 20
   8. Candy cane cocoa bombs................................... 22
   9. Fireball Hot Cocoa Bombs 24
   10. Heart-shaped Cocoa bombs 26
   11. S'mores Hot Cocoa Bombs................................ 28
   12. Skellington Hot Cocoa Bombs 30
   13. Fruity Pebbles Hot Cocoa Bombs 33
   14. Marshmallow Chocolate Bombs....................... 36
   15. Cappuccino Bombs... 39
   16. Creamed Coffee Bombs 41
   17. Blonde White Mocha Coffee Bomb 43
   18. Black Forest Coffee Bomb................................ 45
   19. Spicy Mexican Mocha Bomb 47
   20. Raspberry Frappuccino Bomb 49
   21. Bulletproof Coffee Bombs 51
   22. Instant Orange Cappuccino 53
   23. Floral Tea Bomb 55
   24. Tea Bomb with Vanilla Syrup 57
   25. Black Chai Tea Bombs....................................... 59
   26. Sugar Tea bombs 61
   27. Rose Hips Green Tea Bomb 63
   28. Coconut Chai Spritzer Bomb 65
   29. Irish Crème Coffee Bombs Recipe 67
   30. Fruit tea Bomb 69

31. Earl Grey Tea Bombs 71
32. Sugar-free tea bombs 74
33. Colored Hot Tea Bombs 76
34. Herbal Tea Bombs 79
35. Cocktail fizzer 82
36. Cosmopolitan Fizzy Bombs 84
37. Tequila Sunrise Fizzy Bombs 86
38. Strawberry Mimosa 88
39. Bloody Mary 90
40. Margarita Magic Bomb 92
41. Coconut Mojito 94
42. Piña Colada Bomb 96
43. Pineapple Guava 98
44. Fizzy Spicy Beer Bomb 100
45. Bellini Blush 102
46. Lavender Lush bomb 104
47. Hangover Charcoal bomb 106
48. Limoncello Fizzer 108
49. Old Fashioned 110
50. Bubblegum Bomb 112
51. Birthday Cake 114
52. Bee's Knees 116
53. Berry Smash 118
54. Strawberry Basil Mojito 120
55. Grapefruit Crush 122
56. Peaches n' Cream Bombs 124
57. Blueberry Bombs 127
58. Cucumber Mint Twist 130
59. Cotton Candy Glitter Bombs 132
60. Koolaid Bombs 134
61. Caramel Apple Cider Bombs 136
62. Candy floss bomb 138
63. Azalea bomb 140

64. Mango batida bomb 142
65. Frosted cranberry bomb 144
66. Blue raspberry bomb 146
67. Raspberry orange bomb... 148
68. Lemon drop bomb 150
69. Cosmo Bomb 152
70. Peacharita Bomb 154
71. Passion Hurricane bomb 156
72. Michelada Bomb... 158
73. Zombie Cocktail bomb 160
74. Sazerac Bomb.. 162
75. Mango Mule 164
76. Citrus Fizz 166
77. Virgin Cucumber Bomb 168
78. Ritual apple bomb 170
79. Shirley Ginger 172
80. Watermelon Margarita 174
81. Berry Burlesque 176
82. Lavender Lemonade 178
83. Rosemary Blueberry Smash.. 180
84. Coconut, Cucumber & Mint Bomb................................... 182
85. Watermelon & Mint bomb 184
86. Lemongrass & Jasmine bomb 186
87. Blueberry Mojito 188
88. Virgin Paloma 190
89. Wildcat Cooler.. 192
90. Pineapple Ginger Beer Bomb 194
91. Seedlip Spice & Tonic... 196
92. Pineapple Cobbler 198
93. Tahitian Coffee... 200
94. Raspberry Bee's Knees 202
95. Pina Serrano Margarita 204
96. Nopaloma bomb... 206

97. Revitalizer Bomb 208
98. Arnold Palmer's Fizzy Bomb 210
99. Prosecco Rose 212
100. Fruity Drink Bombs 214
CONCLUSION... 216

INTRODUCTION

Are you ready to indulge in the latest sensation taking the world of desserts by storm? Hot chocolate bombs have been popping up all over social media, and for good reason: they are absolutely delicious! These little balls of goodness are filled with hot chocolate mix, marshmallows, and other delectable surprises that burst open when you pour hot milk over them, creating a decadent, creamy cup of cocoa.

In this Hot Chocolate Bombs Cookbook, you will find a wide variety of recipes for all tastes and occasions. Whether you prefer classic hot cocoa flavors or want to experiment with exciting new combinations like mint, peanut butter, or even pumpkin spice, this cookbook has got you covered.

You will learn all the tips and tricks you need to create perfect hot chocolate bombs every time, from the right molds to use to the best chocolate to melt. Impress your friends and family with stunningly decorated bombs, including holiday-themed designs for Christmas, Halloween, and Valentine's Day.

So, grab your apron and get ready to indulge in a chocolatey adventure with this Hot Chocolate Bombs Cookbook!

Hot chocolate bombs, hot cocoa, marshmallows, decadent, creamy, delicious, recipes, classic, new combinations, mint, peanut butter, pumpkin spice, tips, tricks, molds, chocolate, decorated bombs, holiday-themed designs, Christmas, Halloween, Valentine's Day, chocolatey adventure..

1. Matcha Hot chocolate bombs

MAKES: 6 bombs

INGREDIENTS:
MATCHA TRUFFLES
- 1/4 cup white chocolate chips
- 1 tablespoon heavy whipping cream
- 1/4 teaspoon matcha powder

WHITE CHOCOLATE MATCHA SHELL
- 3/4 cup white chocolate chips
- 1 & 1/2 teaspoon matcha powder

EQUIPMENT:
- Half sphere molds

INSTRUCTIONS:
MATCHA TRUFFLES
- ☑ Melt the white chocolate, heavy whipping cream, and matcha powder together in a small microwave-safe bowl for 60 seconds.
- ☑ Cover and refrigerate in the fridge or freezer for 30-45 minutes, or until totally set.
- ☑ Scoop out 1 teaspoon at a time, roll, and place on a platter.

MATCHA SHELLS
- ☑ In a medium mixing bowl, combine the white chocolate and matcha powder. Microwave until melted.
- ☑ When the chocolate is all melted, put a tablespoon of it into each mold cavity.
- ☑ Spread the chocolate mixture along the sides of each mold with the back of a spoon.
- ☑ Freeze the mold for 15 minutes or until the shells are completely firm.

TO ASSEMBLE
- ☑ Place one of the empty chocolate domes on a dish that has been lightly heated. Place the matcha truffle in it, then cook the second half and join them.
- ☑ Melt the remaining white chocolate in a plastic bag and pour it over the matcha hot chocolate bombs lightly.
- ☑ Keep refrigerated in an airtight container for up to a week.

2. Cotton Candy Chocolate Bombs

MAKES: 5 bombs

INGREDIENTS:
- 6 tablespoons strawberry milk mix
- 1 cup of pink candy melts, melted
- Cotton candy
- 1 cup of blue candy melts, melted
- ½ cup of mini marshmallows

EQUIPMENT:
- Silicone mold

INSTRUCTIONS:
- ☑ Fill each half-sphere mold with 1 tablespoon of each color.
- ☑ To create a marble look, stir the colors together with the back of a spoon and distribute them evenly throughout the molds.
- ☑ Put in the refrigerator to set for 8 minutes.
- ☑ Carefully remove the spheres from the mold once they have solidified.
- ☑ Spoon 6 of the spherical halves with 1 tablespoon of strawberry milk.
- ☑ On top, sprinkle some cotton candy and a few little marshmallows.
- ☑ Microwave a small dish for 45 seconds to preheat it.
- ☑ One of the empty sphere halves should be placed on the plate for a brief period to melt the edges, creating glue.
- ☑ Align the corresponding, filled half sphere's
- ☑ Combine with 6 ounces of hot milk or water to serve.

3. Pumpkin Spice Hot Chocolate Bombs

MAKES: 3 bombs

INGREDIENTS:
- 1 1/2 cups white candy melts, melted
- 1/4 cup orange candy melts, melted
- 3 packets Pumpkin Spice Hot Chocolate Mix
- 1/4 cup Mini Marshmallows

EQUIPMENT:
- Silicone Sphere Mold

DIRECTIONS
- Spoon one and a half teaspoons of chocolate into each ball.
- With a spoon or brush, smooth and move the chocolate around the mold to cover it completely.
- Put it in the refrigerator for around five minutes.
- Once the chocolate has hardened, carefully remove it from the molds.
- Add marshmallows to three of the chocolates after adding the hot chocolate mixture.
- Warm up a dish that can be heated in the microwave.
- Place the empty bar of chocolate on the plate, and then melt the edges.
- Adjust it to the top of the full hot chocolate spherical.
- Then, using the chocolate as glue, gently push the pieces together.
- Pour orange chocolate into a piping bag, then add strings to the bomb's top.

4. Hot Chocolate Bombs

MAKES: 4 bombs

INGREDIENTS:
- 2 cups Chocolate chips, melted
- 3 packets of Hot cocoa mix

TOPPINGS
- Mini marshmallows
- Sprinkles
- Toffee pieces

DIRECTIONS
- ☑ Dollop the melted chocolate into the molds with a spoon, smoothing it along the edges until completely coated.
- ☑ Refrigerate the chocolate for about 30 minutes, or until it is completely solid.
- ☑ Fill your mold with the hot cocoa mix and any other ingredients.
- ☑ Pour the remaining chocolate on top of the bombs to seal the "back" of them.
- ☑ Place the mold in the refrigerator until the chocolate has set.
- ☑ Serve the bomb in a mug with hot milk and stir until melted.

5. Rainbow White Hot Chocolate Bombs

MAKES: 12 bombs

INGREDIENTS:
- 16 ounces chopped white chocolate, melted
- ½ cup Mini marshmallows
- 6 white hot chocolate mix packets
- ½ cup Lucky Charms Marshmallows
- Sprinkles

INSTRUCTIONS:
- ☑ Spoon about 1 tablespoon of the melted chocolate into each mold and smooth it out with the back of the spoon.
- ☑ Allow 10 minutes to freeze.
- ☑ Remove the molds from the freezer, and take the chocolate shells out of the molds.
- ☑ Place the halves on a hot flat platter to flatten the edges.
- ☑ Fill each cavity with a packet of marshmallows and hot cocoa mix.
- ☑ Reheat the plate in the microwave for two minutes.
- ☑ Place the remaining parts, one on top of the other, and gently press them together to seal.
- ☑ Serve with a cup of hot milk.

6. Marble Chocolate Egg

MAKES: 3 bombs

INGREDIENTS:
- 10 tablespoons white chocolate, melted
- Assorted candies
- Food coloring

INSTRUCTIONS:
- ☑ To make desired colors, combine 1 tablespoon of melted chocolate with various food colorings.
- ☑ Fill a silicone egg mold halfway with colored chocolate. To make a marbled design, swirl the colors together with a toothpick.
- ☑ Pour molten white chocolate over the top of the mold and rotate it to coat it completely. Allow cooling completely before removing it from the mold.
- ☑ Preheat a metal sheet pan and press one-half of each egg onto it until the edges begin to melt.
- ☑ Fill with different candies as quickly as possible, then press the two parts together until they are completely sealed.

7. Rum Chata Hot Cocoa Bombs

MAKES: 3 bombs

INGREDIENTS:
- 12 Ounces White Melting Chocolate
- 6 Tablespoons Rum Chata
- 2 Packets of Hot Cocoa Mix
- 1 cup Mini Marshmallows
- 6 cups Hot Milk

EQUIPMENT:
- 1 set of Silicone Molds

INSTRUCTIONS:
- ☑ Spoon chocolate into the molds, being sure to coat the insides, and set aside for 15 minutes to harden.
- ☑ Remove the chocolate from the molds.
- ☑ Melt one-half of a ball's edges.
- ☑ Remove, spread out on a cookie sheet, and top with cocoa powder, rum chata, and miniature marshmallows.
- ☑ Melt just the edges of the remaining half of the chocolate balls and set it on top of one of the chocolate balls, filling it with cocoa or other ingredients to create the top of the ball or bomb.
- ☑ After they have been filled and melted together, place the Cocoa Bombs in the refrigerator for 30 minutes, or until the chocolate is completely set.
- ☑ Pour warm milk over top.
- ☑ Add the cocoa powder and then serve!

8. Candy cane cocoa bombs

MAKES: 6 bombs

INGREDIENTS:
- 1/4 cup crushed candy canes
- Mini candy cane sprinkles
- 1/2 cup store-bought cocoa mix
- 12 ounces bright white candy melts, tempered
- 1/2 cup dehydrated mini marshmallows
- 1/4 teaspoon peppermint flavoring oil
- Candy cane-shaped cake toppers
- Peppermint marshmallows

INSTRUCTIONS:
- ☑ Melt the chocolate and season to taste with the flavored oil.
- ☑ Pour 1-2 teaspoons of melted chocolate into each mold and smooth out with a brush or the back of a spoon to ensure that the chocolate covers the entire form and extends up the sides.
- ☑ Set aside for 5 minutes in the refrigerator.
- ☑ Carefully remove the mold.
- ☑ For the tops, set aside 6 of the shells.
- ☑ Melt the edges of the 6 bottom shells.
- ☑ To each shell, add 1 tablespoon of the white cocoa mixture, a generous amount of candy cane sprinkles, a peppermint marshmallow, a candy cane-shaped candy topping, and several dried mini marshmallows.
- ☑ Melt the edges of the tops and attach them to the remaining shells.
- ☑ Savor with hot milk.
- ☑ Store prepared chocolate bombs in an airtight container at room temperature for up to two weeks.

9. Fireball Hot Cocoa Bombs

MAKES: 6 bombs

INGREDIENTS:
- 7 oz milk chocolate melting wafers, melted
- 6 tablespoons hot cocoa mix
- 2 shots of Fireball Whiskey
- Red jimmies
- Gold sprinkle mix
- Semi Sphere silicone mold

INSTRUCTIONS:
- Fill each mold cavity with a spoonful of melted chocolate.
- Use a spoon or pastry brush to evenly distribute chocolate into the cavity of the mold.
- Place in the freezer for five minutes.
- Add the Fireball Whiskey and the hot cocoa mix to a large mixing dish and whisk well.
- Snip the tip off the ziplock bag or pastry bag and pour the remaining melted chocolate into it.
- Microwave a small dish.
- Fill 6 chocolate half-spheres with the Fireball and cocoa mixture.
- Add the Fireball/cocoa mixture to 6 chocolate half-spheres.
- Place an empty half sphere upside down on a heating plate, and slowly move it around to melt the edge.
- Attach to a chocolate half-sphere that has cocoa or fireballs within.
- To serve, add 6 oz of hot water or milk to a mug, stir thoroughly, and then sip.

10. Heart-shaped Cocoa bombs

MAKES: 6 bombs

INGREDIENTS:
HOT CHOCOLATE POWDER:
- ¼ cup chopped white chocolate
- 1 cup superfine sugar
- ½ cup unsweetened cocoa powder
- 2 tablespoons powdered milk

HOT CHOCOLATE BOMBS:
- 1 cup hot chocolate powder
- 16 ounces white chocolate bark, melted
- ¼ cup mini marshmallows

DIRECTIONS
HOT CHOCOLATE POWDER:
- ☑ Combine all of the ingredients for the chocolate powder in a small bowl.

HOT CHOCOLATE BOMBS:
- ☑ Fill each of the heart-shaped mold's holes with 2-3 tablespoons of melted white chocolate using a spoon or a pastry brush.
- ☑ Chill for about 5 minutes, or until totally solid.
- ☑ Take the chocolate shells out of the mold and stuff one side with marshmallows and two tablespoons of hot chocolate powder.
- ☑ Heat a non-stick skillet.
- ☑ Put the rim of the empty shell on the surface for 3 to 5 seconds, or until the edge starts to soften.
- ☑ Gently push the two shells together to create a seal.
- ☑ Put the sealed bomb back in the refrigerator for five minutes so it can set.
- ☑ Serve with a cup of hot milk.

11. S'mores Hot Cocoa Bombs

MAKES: 6 Hot Cocoa Bombs

INGREDIENTS:
- 3 Cups Melted White Chocolate Almond Bark
- 1 1/2 Cups of Hot Cocoa Mix - divided
- Mini Marshmallows - 5 for each Bomb - 30 total
- 1 cup of Chocolate - melted - for top decoration
- Mini Marshmallows - toasted - for the top decoration.
- 1 Sleeve of Graham Crackers - halves
- 3 Hershey's Chocolate bars - broken in pieces at the perforations

INSTRUCTIONS:
- ☑ Place the White Chocolate Almond Bark in a microwave-safe bowl, and microwave at 15-second intervals until the chocolate is melted.   Stir between intervals.
- ☑ Spoon the white chocolate inside the mold, enough to cover the bottom and sides with a thick layer of chocolate.   Let sit at room temperature for about 30 minutes, and then refrigerate for another 30 minutes to completely set the chocolate.
- ☑ Remove from the refrigerator, and fill half of the molds with 1/4 cup of the Hot Cocoa Mix and Mini Marshmallows.
- ☑ Remove the other half of the Chocolate from the molds, gently warm the edges in a small nonstick skillet or hot plate to barely melt the edge of the chocolate, and stick the top of the mold to the bottom of the mold, sealing them with the melted chocolate.
- ☑ Place back in the refrigerator for 30 minutes, to set the chocolate.
- ☑ Remove the chocolate bomb from the refrigerator, drizzle melted chocolate across the S'mores Hot Cocoa Bombs, place a dollop of Chocolate on top and place 3 mini toasted Marshmallows on the top.
- ☑ Place a dollop of Chocolate on top of a Graham Cracker square, and stick the two pieces together.   Place another dollop of Chocolate on top of the Chocolate and stick the Hot Cocoa Bomb to the top.
- ☑ To serve, drop in hot Milk, and let it dissolve, stir and enjoy!

12. Skellington Hot Cocoa Bombs

Makes: 8-10 Hot Cocoa Bombs

INGREDIENTS:
- 1 - 30oz Bag of White Chocolate melting wafers
- 2 Cups of pumpkin spice hot cocoa mix
- 1 Cup mini marshmallows
- 1 bottle of black cookie icing

INSTRUCTIONS:
- ☑ Use a paper towel or clean kitchen towel and wipe the inside of the silicone molds. This will allow your chocolate mold to have a shiny coat on it
- ☑ Using a heat-safe bowl, pour into the bowl and place the remaining melting wafers in the microwave for 45-second intervals. Make sure to stir the chocolate after every 45 seconds until completely melted and smooth
- ☑ Using a spoon, spoon about 1-2 tablespoons of the chocolate into the mold
- ☑ Carefully swirl the chocolate to completely coat the inside of the mold
- ☑ Lightly shake the extra chocolate back into the bowl
- ☑ Place the coated molds into the fridge for 5-10 minutes
- ☑ Remove from the fridge and gently peel the silicone mold back away from the hardened chocolate shell
- ☑ Carefully place the mold onto the cookie sheet
- ☑ Repeat steps with remaining molds
- ☑ You should now have 8 half sphere molds
- ☑ Carefully take the open side of the sphere and place it onto the pan to melt off the uneven edges to create a smooth edging
- ☑ Place the shell back onto the cookie sheet and allow the edge to harden
- ☑ Scoop about 1 Tablespoon of the pumpkin spice hot cocoa mix into the bottom of the sphere mold
- ☑ Place a few mini marshmallows into the shell
- ☑ Place the top of the shell back onto the warm pan to melt the edges for a few seconds

- ☑ Quickly place the melted edges onto the filled shell and gently press down
- ☑ Squeeze the cookie icing into the piping bag and cut the tip off.
- ☑ Carefully pipe the details of Jack Skellington's face.
- ☑ Allow the icing to harden before enjoying it in a glass of steamed milk!

13. Fruity Pebbles Hot Cocoa Bombs

Makes: 6

INGREDIENTS:
- 2 cups vanilla-flavored white melting wafers
- ¼ cup blue candy melts
- ¼ cup purple candy melts
- ¼ cup pink candy melts
- 6 tablespoon strawberry chocolate milk powder
- 1 cup fruity pebbles cereal
- ½ cup mini marshmallows
- Half-sphere silicone mold
- Pastry brush

INSTRUCTIONS:
- ☑ In a medium-sized, microwave-safe bowl, melt the white melting wafers in 30-second increments, stirring in between to prevent burning. This should only take 60-90 seconds.
- ☑ Once melted, evenly coat each mold with about 2 tablespoons using your pastry brush or spoon.
- ☑ Once the molds are coated, place them into the refrigerator for about 10-15 minutes until the chocolate has hardened.
- ☑ Remove from fridge and apply a second layer of chocolate and let set again. Then gently remove each half sphere from the mold and set aside.
- ☑ In 3 small, microwave-safe bowls, melt each of the colored candy melts in 30-second increments, stirring between. This should only take about 30-60 seconds.
- ☑ Separate 6 of the sphere halves and reserve the other 6 for the bottoms. One at a time, take the six tops, and using the pastry brush, brush a thin layer of colored candy and melt over the outside of each half sphere.
- ☑ Quickly dip into the fruity pebbles or gently press cereal onto the half sphere and let sit until hardened.
- ☑ In the other 6 plain white halves, spoon in 1 tablespoon of strawberry chocolate milk powder. Top with ½ tablespoon or

more of the fruity pebbles cereal and several mini marshmallows.
- ☑ Warm a small, microwave-safe plate in the microwave for about 45-60 seconds. Place the empty, "painted" half on the warm plate for a few seconds to let the edge melt. The warm, melted edge acts as glue.
- ☑ Immediately place it on top of the coordinating, filled half sphere. Run a clean finger along the edge to clean it up. Finish connecting the other 5 spheres.
- ☑ Serve and enjoy or package and use as gifts!

14. Marshmallow Chocolate Bombs

Make: 8 bombs

INGREDIENTS:
- 6 ounces chopped chocolate or chocolate chips
- 1 ½ tablespoon cocoa powder
- 1 ½ tablespoon granulated sugar
- 1/4 cup dehydrated marshmallow bits
- 1/4 cup chopped contrasting chocolate for drizzling

INSTRUCTIONS:
- ☑ Melt 4 ounces (about 2/3 cup) of the chocolate, then pour 1 teaspoon of melted chocolate into each of the 16 cups in a silicone mold.
- ☑ Use the back of a small spoon, such as a 1/4-teaspoon measuring spoon, to push the melted chocolate up the sides and around the edges of each cup to cover it completely.
- ☑ Melt the remaining 2 ounces (1/3 cup) of chocolate and repeat the process. This time, only pour 1/2 teaspoon melted chocolate into each cup and work with one mold cup at a time, pouring in the chocolate and spreading it on the sides and edges, as it will harden quickly as it comes into contact with the frozen chocolate. It's important to make sure the sides of your mold are well coated and you have a nice thick layer of chocolate—this will help prevent cracking.
- ☑ Freeze the mold(s) for another 5 minutes.
- ☑ Whisk the cocoa powder and granulated sugar together in a small bowl to make a hot chocolate mix. Line a small rimmed baking sheet with parchment paper and top with an upside-down wire rack. This will keep the chocolate shells from rolling around while you're filling them.
- ☑ Remove the chocolate shells from the molds. It's a tricky process, so take your time. Use your thumbs to gently peel the silicone away from the edges of the chocolate, then push up from the bottom of the mold with your index fingers to help lift the shell out.

- ☑ If there are slight cracks or jagged edges on the shell, don't worry. They will be smoothed out in the next step.
- ☑ Fill the hot chocolate bombs:
- ☑ Heat a microwave-safe plate in the microwave just until warm, about 30 seconds. Place 1 chocolate shell, open-side down, on the warm plate, and melt the edges until flat.
- ☑ Carefully spoon 1/2 teaspoon cocoa-sugar mixture into the shell. Place the filled shell on the rack to hold it upright.
- ☑ Carefully press the two halves together.
- ☑ Use your finger to spread the melted chocolate around the seam of the bomb to seal it closed. Repeat until all the bombs are filled and sealed.
- ☑ To decorate, melt the white chocolate and place it in a small zip-top sandwich bag. Snip a small corner off the bag, then drizzle the chocolate over the bombs. This helps cover up any unsightly seams or fingerprint marks as well!
- ☑ Heat 3/4 cup milk in a microwave-safe mug or a saucepan over medium-low heat just until steaming hot.
- ☑ Gently drop a hot chocolate bomb into the mug or pour the steaming milk over a bomb placed in a mug and watch the magic happen.
- ☑ Serve with additional marshmallow bits, if desired.

15. Cappuccino Bombs

MAKES: 6 bombs

INGREDIENTS:
- Chocolate candy wafers, melted
- 1 tablespoon + 1 teaspoon Cappuccino instant mix
- Vanilla white candy wafers, melted
- Hot Milk

EQUIPMENT:
- Medium Semi-sphere silicone mold

INSTRUCTIONS:
- ☑ Using the back of a spoon, fill the silicone molds with melted chocolate.
- ☑ Refrigerate or freeze for 10-15 minutes, or until they're easy to remove.
- ☑ Add 1 tablespoon + 1 teaspoon instant cappuccino mix to one chocolate half.
- ☑ In the microwave, heat a plate for around 15 seconds. To melt the chocolate, take the other chocolate half and place the open part onto the hot plate for a few seconds.
- ☑ Connect the two halves of the chocolates and seal them together.
- ☑ Enjoy with hot milk.

16. Creamed Coffee Bombs

MAKES: 3 bombs

INGREDIENTS:
- ½ cups Isomalt, melted
- 3-4 teaspoons of Instant Coffee
- ¼ cups Powdered Coffee Creamer
- Brown Gel Food Coloring

INSTRUCTIONS:
- ☑ Coat one half-sphere mold in brown food coloring and 1 tablespoon of melted Isomalt.
- ☑ With the bottom of your spoon, push the isomalt up the sides of the mold.
- ☑ Freeze the bomb molds filled with Isomalt for 5 minutes. Peel the silicone from the molds after removing them from the freezer from the Isomalt cup with a gentle peeling motion.
- ☑ To Isomalt molds, add 1 tablespoon of instant coffee and powdered creamer.
- ☑ Heat a plate and press one of the empty Isomalt cups open-side-down onto the flat section of the heating plate for about 10 seconds.
- ☑ Place this edge on top of one of the filled cups right away.
- ☑ This will join the two halves of the bomb.

17. Blonde White Mocha Coffee Bomb

MAKES: 3 bombs

INGREDIENTS:
- 1 cup white chocolate chips, melted
- 6 tablespoons vanilla powdered coffee creamer

INSTRUCTIONS:
- ☑ Coat the inside of the silicone mold with an even layer of chocolate using a spoon or pastry brush.
- ☑ Freeze the mold for 10-15 minutes in the freezer.
- ☑ Carefully remove the half circles from the mold and lay them on a frozen platter.
- ☑ Spoon 1-2 teaspoons of coffee creamer, together with any additional ingredients into three half spheres.
- ☑ Lightly heat the edges of the remaining sphere halves and lay them on top of the creamer-holding ones.
- ☑ To use the coffee bomb, place it in a coffee mug and pour hot coffee over it.

18. Black Forest Coffee Bomb

MAKES: 2 bombs

INGREDIENTS:
- ½ cups Isomalt, melted
- 3-4 teaspoons of Instant Coffee
- 2 tablespoons Chocolate syrup
- Shaved chocolate

EQUIPMENT:
- 1 set of Silicone Molds

INSTRUCTIONS:
- ☑ With the bottom of your spoon, push the isomalt up the sides of the mold.
- ☑ Freeze the bomb molds for 5 minutes.
- ☑ Peel the silicone from the molds after removing them from the freezer.
- ☑ To each Isomalt bomb, add instant coffee, chocolate syrup, and Shaved chocolate.
- ☑ Heat a plate and press one of the empty Isomalt cups open-side-down onto the flat section of the heating plate.
- ☑ Place this warmed edge Isomalt on top of one of the filled cups right away.
- ☑ This will join the two halves of the bomb.

19. Spicy Mexican Mocha Bomb

MAKES: 2 bombs

INGREDIENTS:
- ½ cups Isomalt, melted
- 3-4 teaspoons of Instant Coffee
- 1/4 teaspoon Vietnamese Cassia Cinnamon
- ¼ cups Powdered Coffee Creamer
- 1/4 teaspoon Jamaican Allspice
- 1/8 teaspoon Cayenne Pepper
- 2 tablespoons Powdered Sugar
- 1 tablespoon Unsweetened ground chocolate powder

EQUIPMENT:
- 1 set of Silicone Molds

INSTRUCTIONS:
- ☑ With the bottom of your spoon, push the isomalt up the sides of the mold.
- ☑ Freeze the bomb molds for 5 minutes.
- ☑ Peel the silicone from the molds after removing them from the freezer.
- ☑ To each Isomalt bomb, add instant coffee, powdered creamer, Powdered Sugar, chocolate powder, Cinnamon, Jamaican Allspice, and Cayenne Pepper.
- ☑ Heat a plate and press one of the empty Isomalt cups open-side-down onto the flat section of the heating plate.
- ☑ Place this warmed edge Isomalt on top of one of the filled cups right away.
- ☑ This will join the two halves of the bomb.

20. Raspberry Frappuccino Bomb

MAKES: 2 bombs

INGREDIENTS:
- ½ cups Isomalt, melted
- 3-4 teaspoons of Instant Coffee
- ¼ cups Powdered Coffee Creamer
- 2 tablespoons raspberry syrup
- 3 tablespoons chocolate syrup

EQUIPMENT:
- 1 set of Silicone Molds

INSTRUCTIONS:
- ☑ With the bottom of your spoon, push the isomalt up the sides of the mold.
- ☑ Freeze the bomb molds for 5 minutes. Peel the silicone from the molds after removing them from the freezer.
- ☑ To each Isomalt bomb, add instant coffee, Powdered Coffee Creamer, raspberry syrup, and chocolate syrup.
- ☑ Heat a plate and press one of the empty Isomalt cups open-side-down onto the flat section of the heating plate.
- ☑ Place this warmed edge Isomalt on top of one of the filled cups right away.
- ☑ This will join the two halves of the bomb.

21. **Bulletproof Coffee Bombs**

MAKES: 3 bombs

INGREDIENTS:
- 1/3 cup ghee
- 3 scoops collagen
- 1.5 Tablespoons coconut oil or MCT oil, Melted
- 1/4 teaspoon cinnamon
- 1 teaspoon cocoa powder

INSTRUCTIONS:
- ☑ Using the back of a spoon, coat 6 half-globe molds with roughly 1 tablespoon of melted ghee.
- ☑ Freeze the mold for approximately 10 minutes.
- ☑ Set the hardened shells on the cooling plate after removing them from the molds. Half of the molds should be filled with collagen and cinnamon.
- ☑ Gently dip the unfilled half shells in the melted coconut oil. Place it face-down on top of a filled half shell, then close the edges by rubbing your fingertips around the entire sealed region.
- ☑ Return it to the freezer for another 5-10 minutes.
- ☑ In a separate bowl, whisk together the cocoa powder and the remaining melted coconut oil until smooth.
- ☑ Drizzle 1/2-1 teaspoon of the mixture over the ghee balls and season with sea salt. Place back in the freezer until ready to use.
- ☑ Serve with a cup of hot coffee that has been freshly brewed.

22. Instant Orange Cappuccino

MAKES: 2 bombs

INGREDIENTS:
- ½ cups Isomalt, melted
- 3-4 teaspoons of Instant Coffee
- ¼ cups Powdered Coffee Creamer
- 1/3 cup Sugar
- 1 or 2 orange hard candies (crushed)

EQUIPMENT:
- 1 set of Silicone Molds

INSTRUCTIONS:
- ☑ With the bottom of your spoon, push the isomalt up the sides of the mold.
- ☑ Freeze the bomb molds for 5 minutes. Peel the silicone from the molds after removing them from the freezer.
- ☑ To each Isomalt bomb, add instant coffee, powdered creamer, sugar, and orange candies.
- ☑ Heat a plate and press one of the empty Isomalt cups open-side-down onto the flat section of the heating plate.
- ☑ Place this warmed edge Isomalt on top of one of the filled cups right away.
- ☑ This will join the two halves of the bomb.

23. Floral Tea Bomb

MAKES: 3 bombs

INGREDIENTS:
- 3 Tea bags or loose-leaf tea
- 1/2 cup Isomalt Crystals, melted
- Dried Edible Flowers

EQUIPMENT:
- Semi Sphere Silicone Mold
- Saucepan

INSTRUCTIONS:
- ☑ Pour a tablespoon or two of melted isomalt into each side of the globe, swirling the mixture around to cover the entire surface.
- ☑ Set aside for 30 minutes to allow the orbs to cool.
- ☑ In one of the orbs, place a tea bag and then add dried flowers.
- ☑ Remove the empty globes with care and place a small skillet over low heat. One of the crystals' edges should be melted just enough to act as an adhesive.
- ☑ Combine the two tea globes to form a sphere.
- ☑ Top with edible flowers by delicately dipping the flower in the Isomalt mixture and attaching it to the top with sugar gloves.

24. Tea Bomb with Vanilla Syrup

MAKES: 3 bombs

INGREDIENTS:
- 1 cup powdered erythritol
- 1/3 cup sugar-free vanilla syrup
- 2 tablespoons water
- Food coloring
- Loose tea or tea bags

EQUIPMENT:
- Silicon half-moon mold

INSTRUCTIONS:
- ☑ In a medium saucepan, combine the powdered sweetener, syrup, and water. Heat over medium-high heat until the temperature reaches 300°F.
- ☑ Take the pan off the heat. If desired, add a few drops of food coloring.
- ☑ Pour roughly 1-2 tablespoons of the liquid candy mixture into one of the mold's cavities and spread it out with a spoon along the sides.
- ☑ Peel the candy out from the silicone mold once it has solidified. Six of the half-moons should be filled with loose tea or a tea bag.
- ☑ Heat a skillet over medium heat to bind the two parts together. With no tea in the skillet, melt the corners of a half-moon. Then immediately place the other half on top of the tea to seal it.

25. Black Chai Tea Bombs

MAKES: 2 bombs

INGREDIENTS:
- ¼ cup Isomalt, melted
- 2 Black Chai Tea Bags

INSTRUCTIONS:
- ☑ Pour about a quarter of the melted isomalt into the spherical mold cavity, pressing the isomalt up and around the mold's edges with your spoon.
- ☑ Freeze the filled molds for 5 minutes to solidify them.
- ☑ Take the full molds out of the freezer and gently pull the mold away from the half-spheres of isomalt.
- ☑ Insert a tea bag between two isomalt half-spheres, leaving the tea bomb's tag hanging out.
- ☑ Preheat your saucepan over medium heat, then turn an empty isomalt half-sphere over and press the flat edge of the isomalt form against the pan's bottom until it begins to melt.
- ☑ Place the slightly melted isomalt half on top of an isomalt half-bomb containing a tea bag as soon as possible.
- ☑ When the isomalt cools, the two sides of the tea bomb will seal together in a matter of seconds.

26. Sugar Tea bombs

MAKES: 7 bombs

INGREDIENTS:
- 2 tablespoons water
- 1 cup white sugar
- 1/3 cup Light Corn Syrup
- 7 tea bags
- Gel food coloring
- Luster dust or dried flowers

INSTRUCTIONS:
- ☑ In a stove saucepan, combine the sugar, water, and light corn syrup.
- ☑ Bring to a boil.
- ☑ Stir in the gel food coloring.
- ☑ Pour the sugar into a silicon mold and spread it around with the back of a spoon. Allow 15-20 minutes for the mixture to fully solidify.
- ☑ Once the sugar is set, carefully lift the bottom of the mold to release the circle, and carefully remove half of the pieces from the mold, leaving half of the sugar circles in place.
- ☑ Place tea bags, flowers, and/or luster dust in the semi-circles you left in the mold.
- ☑ Extract the tea bag thread from the mold.
- ☑ Preheat the stove under the skillet on low for a few seconds.
- ☑ Smooth half of the circular mold into the skillet and heat the rim.
- ☑ Place the sugar circle back on top and carefully seal both sides together
- ☑ Set them aside and secure them for another 5-10 minutes.
- ☑ Carefully pop the tea bombs out of the mold by gently pressing on the bottom, holding the bomb on top, and removing it.

27. Rose Hips Green Tea Bomb

MAKES: 7 bombs

INGREDIENTS:
- 2 tablespoons water
- 1 cup white sugar
- 1 lemon, squeezed, seeds removed
- Gel food coloring
- tea bags
- 1/3 cup Light Corn Syrup
- 2 Tablespoons organic Rose hips
- 1-2 pinches of cayenne

INSTRUCTIONS:
- ☑ In a stove saucepan, combine the sugar, water, lemon juice, and light corn syrup.
- ☑ Bring to a boil.
- ☑ Stir in the gel food coloring.
- ☑ Pour the sugar into a silicon mold and spread it around with the back of a spoon. Allow 15-20 minutes for the mixture to fully solidify.
- ☑ Once the sugar is set, carefully lift the bottom of the mold to release the circle, and carefully remove half of the pieces from the mold, leaving half of the sugar circles in place.
- ☑ Place tea bags, Rose hips, and cayenne in the semi-circles you left in the mold.
- ☑ Preheat the stove under the skillet on low for a few seconds.
- ☑ Smooth half of the circular mold into the skillet and heat the rim.
- ☑ Place the sugar circle back on top and carefully seal both sides together
- ☑ Set them aside and secure them for another 5-10 minutes.
- ☑ Carefully pop the tea bombs out of the mold by gently pressing on the bottom, holding the bomb on top, and removing it.

28. Coconut Chai Spritzer Bomb

MAKES: 2 bombs

INGREDIENTS:
- ¼ cup Isomalt, melted
- ¼ cup of Coconut Chia Tea
- 2 drops of Stevia

INSTRUCTIONS:
- ☑ Pour about a quarter of the melted isomalt into the spherical mold cavity, pressing the isomalt up and around the mold's edges with your spoon.
- ☑ Freeze the filled molds for 5 minutes to solidify them.
- ☑ Take the full molds out of the freezer and gently pull the mold away from the half-spheres of isomalt.
- ☑ Pour the chia tea into the mold, along with 1 drop of stevia.
- ☑ Preheat your saucepan over medium heat, then turn an empty isomalt half-sphere over and press the flat edge of the isomalt form against the pan's bottom until it begins to melt.
- ☑ Place the somewhat melted isomalt half on top of the chia tea-filled isomalt half-bomb right away. When the isomalt cools, the two sides of the tea bomb will seal together in a matter of seconds.
- ☑ Serve the bomb with a glass of mineral water.

29. Irish Crème Coffee Bombs Recipe

MAKES: 3 bombs

INGREDIENTS:
- 1 ½ cups white chocolate chips, melted
- 1 tablespoon brown sugar
- 6 tablespoons vanilla coffee creamer powder
- 3 tablespoons whiskey
- 36 oz brewed coffee

INSTRUCTIONS:
- ☑ Spread the melted chocolate into the cavity of the sphere silicone mold with a spoon.
- ☑ Freeze the mold for 15 minutes before using it.
- ☑ Remove the molds from the freezer and carefully remove each half-sphere from the mold, placing them on the frozen plate.
- ☑ In three of the spheres, combine the brown sugar, coffee creamer, and whiskey.
- ☑ Slightly melt or heat the edges of the remaining three sections and push them together to form a circle. To fix the seam, you can use more melted chocolate and pipe down the edge.
- ☑ Refrigerate or keep on the counter in an airtight container until ready to serve.
- ☑ To serve, put the bomb in a mug and top it with hot poured coffee. As the chocolate melts, stir to incorporate everything.

30. Fruit tea Bomb

MAKES: 1 bomb

INGREDIENTS:
- 1 cup powdered erythritol
- 2 tablespoons water
- 2 tablespoons Lipton instant tea
- Fresh mint
- ¼ cup Lemon juice
- 1/3 cup sugar-free vanilla syrup
- ¼ cup White grape juice
- ⅔ cup Sugar

INSTRUCTIONS:
- ☑ In a medium saucepan, combine the powdered sweetener, syrup, and water. Heat until the temperature reaches 300°F.
- ☑ Pour roughly 1-2 tablespoons of the liquid candy mixture into one of the mold's cavities and spread it out with a spoon along the sides.
- ☑ Peel the candy out from the silicone mold once it has solidified.
- ☑ Fill six of the half-moons should be filled with loose tea or a tea bag.
- ☑ Heat a skillet over medium heat to bind the two parts together. With no tea in the skillet, melt the corners of a half-moon. Then immediately place the other half on top of the tea to seal it.

31. Earl Grey Tea Bombs

Makes: 2

INGREDIENTS:
- 1/2 cup Isomalt
- 2 Individual Earl Grey Tea Bags
- 2 tablespoons Dried Lavender Blossoms

INSTRUCTIONS:
MAKE THE TEA BOMB
- ☑ Place isomalt into a heat-safe measuring cup. Microwave per the directions on the package until completely melted.
- ☑ Add about ¼ of the melted isomalt to one spherical mold cavity, using your spoon to press the isomalt up and around the edges of the mold. Repeat with 3 additional molds.
- ☑ Put the filled molds into the freezer for 5 minutes to harden.
- ☑ Remove the filled molds from the freezer and gently peel the mold away from the isomalt half-spheres.
- ☑ Place a teabag into two of the isomalt half-spheres, leaving the tag of the tea bomb hanging out.
- ☑ Add 1 tablespoon of the lavender blossoms into each of the tea bomb halves with the tea bags.
- ☑ Heat a plate in the microwave until it's hot to the touch, turn an empty isomalt half-sphere over and rub the flat edge of the isomalt shape onto the bottom of the plate until it just starts to melt.
- ☑ Immediately place the slightly melted isomalt half on top of an isomalt half-bomb with a teabag inside. The two sides of the tea bomb will seal together in just a moment or two when the isomalt cools.
- ☑ When you're ready to drink your tea, simply place the tea bomb into your mug, then pour hot water over it. The tea bomb will melt and the tea bag will steep. Isomalt is not overly sweet, so you may want to add some sweetener if you prefer a sweet cup of tea.

TO MAKE A LONDON FOG
- ☑ Place your tea bomb in a mug.

- ☑ Pour 6 oz of water over the top, to melt the bomb & start steeping your tea.
- ☑ Warm ¼ cup of milk & froth, if desired.
- ☑ You can add a little sugar to the warm milk if you prefer sweeter tea.
- ☑ Pour the warm milk in to fill your cup.

32. Sugar-free tea bombs

Makes: 2

INGREDIENTS:
- 1 cup sugar-free sweetener of choice
- 1/3 cup sugar-free syrup
- 2 tablespoons water
- food coloring
- loose tea or tea bags of choice
- silicone half-moon molds

INSTRUCTIONS:
- ☑ To a medium saucepan, add sweetener, syrup, and water. Heat over medium-high heat until a candy thermometer reaches 300°F (about 5 minutes once boiling).
- ☑ Remove from heat. Add food coloring if using.
- ☑ Working quickly, add about 1-2 tablespoons in a cavity of the mold and spoon up along the edges. Keeping pushing the liquid up until it hardens. A brush works well too. Work with 2 cavities at a time. Repeat with remaining molds.
- ☑ Once hardened, peel away from the mold. To six of the half-moons, add tea or a tea bag.
- ☑ Heat a skillet over medium heat. To the six half-moons with no tea, melt the edges on the skillet. Then quickly place the on top of the other half with the tea to seal. Repeat with the remaining balls.
- ☑ To use, place the tea bomb in a large cup. Slowly pour hot water over the tea bomb and watch it explode out of the tea leaves.

33. <u>Colored Hot Tea Bombs</u>

Makes: 2

INGREDIENTS:
- Isomalt Crystals
- Gel Food Coloring
- Tea of choice
- Dried Edible Flowers, herbs, or sugar cubes
- 1 Small Saucepan
- 1 Large Cavity Semi-Sphere Silicone Mold

INSTRUCTIONS:
- ☑ Place isomalt crystals into a small saucepan over medium-high heat.
- ☑ Allow crystals to melt. If needed, shake the pan to facilitate melting. DO NOT STIR.
- ☑ When all crystals have melted, work quickly to spoon the mixture into semi-sphere molds. Be very careful to avoid contact with the skin. This will be hot.
- ☑ Add a few drops of gel food coloring into each mold.
- ☑ Stir with a small spoon to mix with melted crystals.
- ☑ Using the back of the spoon, quickly spread the mixture to cover the entire surface of the mold. Do this step as fast as you can, it won't take long for the mixture to begin to set up.
- ☑ Allow halves to set up before continuing, approximately 30 minutes.
- ☑ Remove the top half of the sphere from the mold by carefully pushing it up from the bottom of the mold. Leave the bottom half in the mold for now.   This makes it easier to assemble the globe.
- ☑ Place tea in the bottom half of the globe in the mold along with any edible flowers, sugar cubes, or herbs you are using. If desired, leave the tea bag string outside the mold.
- ☑ Place a small skillet over low heat. This will be used to smooth globe edges and ease joining the two globes together.

- ☑ Place the globe top onto a hot skillet for a few seconds to smooth and melt the edge. Quickly join the bottom globe that is still in the mold.
- ☑ Allow cooling for 5-10 minutes. After a few minutes, you should be able to remove the entire sphere from the mold by carefully pressing up on the mold to release the bottom half of the globe.
- ☑ When ready, put the tea bomb into a heat-safe mug and pour hot water over the top. Stir and enjoy!

34. Herbal Tea Bombs

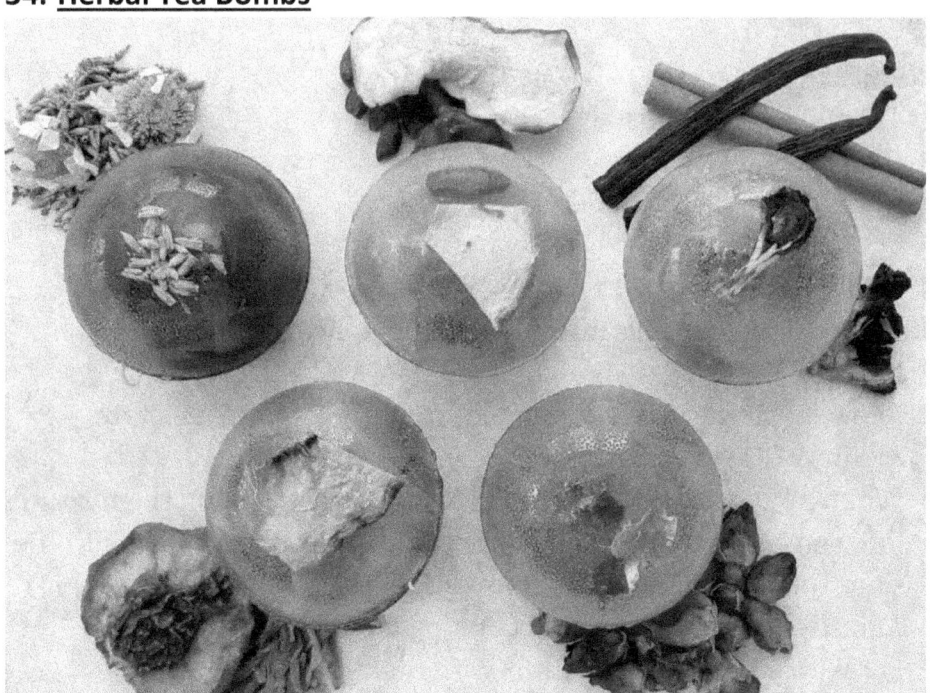

Makes: 2

INGREDIENTS:
- 1/3 cup Isomalt Crystals
- Gel Food Coloring
- Herbal Tea

INSTRUCTIONS:
- ☑ Place isomalt crystals into a small saucepan over medium-high heat.
- ☑ Allow crystals to melt. If needed, shake the pan to facilitate melting. DO NOT STIR.
- ☑ When all crystals have melted, work quickly to spoon the mixture into semi-sphere molds. Be very careful to avoid contact with the skin. This will be hot and can cause severe burns.
- ☑ Add a few drops of gel food coloring into each mold.
- ☑ Stir with a small spoon to mix with melted crystals.
- ☑ Using the back of the spoon, quickly spread the mixture to cover the entire surface of the mold. Do this step as fast as you can, it won't take long for the mixture to begin to set up.
- ☑ Allow halves to set up before continuing, approximately 30 minutes.
- ☑ Remove the top half of the sphere from the mold by carefully pushing it up from the bottom of the mold. Leave the bottom half in the mold for now.   This makes it easier to assemble the globe.
- ☑ Place tea in the bottom half of the globe in the mold along with any edible flowers, sugar cubes, or herbs you are using. If desired, leave the tea bag string outside the mold.
- ☑ Place a small skillet over low heat. This will be used to smooth globe edges and ease joining the two globes together.
- ☑ Place the globe top onto a hot skillet for a few seconds to smooth and melt the edge. Quickly join the bottom globe that is still in the mold.

- ☑ Allow cooling for 5-10 minutes. After a few minutes, you should be able to remove the entire sphere from the mold by carefully pressing up on the mold to release the bottom half of the globe.
- ☑ When ready, put the tea bomb into a heat-safe mug and pour hot water over the top. Stir and enjoy!

35. Cocktail fizzer

MAKES: 10 bombs

INGREDIENTS:
- 1/2 cup Citric acid
- 1 cup Sugar
- 15 ml Assorted bitters
- 1 cup baking soda
- 5g Gum acacia
- Pinch Gold luster
- Water

INSTRUCTIONS:
- ☑ Measure all ingredients into a bowl.
- ☑ Work the mixture with your hands until it has a sandy texture.
- ☑ Make the mixture into balls and put them into a mold to set.
- ☑ Unmold, then store in the refrigerator or on the counter in an airtight container.

36. Cosmopolitan Fizzy Bombs

Makes: 10 Bombs

INGREDIENTS:
- ½ cup ultrafine pure cane sugar
- ½ cup powdered sugar
- 2 teaspoon baking soda
- 2 teaspoon cranberry-raspberry liquid mix-in water enhancer
- 2 teaspoon edible flowers, coarsely chopped
- 6 ounces of orange sparkling water
- ¾ ounces lime-flavored vodka
- ¾ ounces cranberry-flavored vodka
- Edible flowers, for garnish

EQUIPMENT
- Small bowl
- Rimmed tray
- 10-ounce coupe cocktail glass

INSTRUCTIONS:
- ☑ Combine ultrafine sugar, powdered sugar, and baking soda in a small bowl. Stir in water enhancer liquid until the sugar resembles wet sand.
- ☑ Stir in chopped edible flower.
- ☑ Press the mixture into 2 (1 teaspoon) rounded measuring spoons, leaving some excess at top of the spoons. Invert one spoon on top of the other.
- ☑ Press spoons together and shake lightly.
- ☑ Remove one spoon and invert the bomb into your hand.
- ☑ Remove the remaining spoon and place the bomb on a rimmed tray. Repeat with the remaining mixture.
- ☑ Let dry for 4 hours before serving.
- ☑ Store covered at room temperature for up to 2 days.
- ☑ To serve, combine orange sparkling water, lime-flavored vodka, and cranberry-flavored vodka in a 10-ounces coupe cocktail glass.
- ☑ Add one dried bomb; stir to mix well.

37. Tequila Sunrise Fizzy Bombs

Makes: 10 Bombs

INGREDIENTS:
- ½ cup ultrafine pure cane sugar
- ½ cup powdered sugar
- 2 teaspoon baking soda
- 2 teaspoon grenadine syrup
- 2 teaspoon Over the Top rosy red sanding sugar
- 3 ounces 100% orange juice
- 3 ounces of club soda
- 1 ½ ounces gold tequila
- Orange slices, for garnish

EQUIPMENT
- Small bowl
- 2 (1 teaspoon) measures
- Rimmed tray
- 10-ounces cocktail glass

INSTRUCTIONS:
- ☑ Combine ultrafine sugar, powdered sugar, and baking soda in a small bowl.
- ☑ Stir in grenadine until the sugar resembles wet sand. Stir in red sanding sugar.
- ☑ Press the mixture into 2 rounded measuring spoons, leaving some excess at top of the spoons.
- ☑ Invert one spoon on top of the other.
- ☑ Press spoons together and shake lightly.
- ☑ Remove one spoon and invert the bomb into your hand.
- ☑ Remove the remaining spoon and place the bomb on a rimmed tray.
- ☑ Let dry for 4 hours before serving.
- ☑ Store covered at room temperature for up to 2 days.
- ☑ To serve, combine orange juice, club soda, and tequila in a 10-ounces cocktail glass.
- ☑ Add one dried bomb; stir to mix well.

38. Strawberry Mimosa

MAKES: 10 bombs

INGREDIENTS:
- 6 ounces of orange juice
- 6 ounces of strawberry syrup
- 1/2 cup Citric acid
- Water
- 5g Gum acacia
- 1 cup baking soda
- 1 cup Sugar

INSTRUCTIONS:
- ☑ Measure all ingredients into a bowl.
- ☑ Work the mixture with your hands until it has a sandy texture.
- ☑ Form the mixture into balls and place it in a mold.
- ☑ Unmold, then store in the refrigerator or on the counter in an airtight container.

39. **Bloody Mary**

MAKES: 10 bombs

INGREDIENTS:
DRY INGREDIENTS
- 1 teaspoon ground black pepper
- 5g Gum acacia
- 1/2 cup Citric acid
- 1 teaspoon celery salt
- 1 cup baking soda
- 1 cup Sugar

WET INGREDIENTS
- 4 ounces tomato juice or V-8 juice
- 4 ounces of lemon juice
- 4 ounces Worcestershire sauce
- Tabasco sauce to taste
- Water

INSTRUCTIONS:
- ☑ Measure dry ingredients into a bowl.
- ☑ Mix in wet ingredients with your hands, until the mixture has turned into a sand consistency.
- ☑ Form the mixture into balls and place it in a mold.
- ☑ Unmold, then store in the refrigerator or on the counter in an airtight container.

40. Margarita Magic Bomb

MAKES: 8 bombs

INGREDIENTS:
- Good quality Water
- 1/2 cup Citric acid
- 1/8 teaspoon salt
- Zest from half a lime
- 1 cup lime juice
- 1 cup baking soda
- 1 cup Granulated Sugar
- 5g Gum acacia

INSTRUCTIONS:
- ☑ Measure all ingredients into a bowl.
- ☑ Work the mixture with your hands until it has a sandy texture.
- ☑ Form the mixture into balls and place it in a mold.
- ☑ Serve with 1/2 cup Cointreau or orange juice and zest

41. Coconut Mojito

MAKES: 20 bombs

INGREDIENTS:
- 6 ounces of Mint syrup
- 8 ounces of Lime Juice
- 1 cup baking soda
- 1 cup Sugar
- 1/2 cup Citric acid
- 5g Gum acacia
- Water

INSTRUCTIONS:
- ☑ Measure all ingredients into a bowl.
- ☑ Work the mixture with your hands until it has a sandy texture.
- ☑ Form the mixture into balls and place it in a mold.
- ☑ Unmold, then store in the refrigerator or on the counter in an airtight container.

42. Piña Colada Bomb

MAKES: 10 bombs

INGREDIENTS:
- 1 cream of coconut
- ¾ cup pineapple juice
- 3 tablespoons lime juice
- 1/2 cup Citric acid
- 1 cup Sugar
- 5g Gum acacia
- 1/4 Baking soda
- Water

INSTRUCTIONS:
- ☑ Measure all ingredients into a bowl.
- ☑ Work the mixture with your hands until it has a sandy texture.
- ☑ Form the mixture into balls and place it in a mold.

43. Pineapple Guava

MAKES: 10 bombs

INGREDIENTS:
- 4 ounces of Guava Juice
- 4 ounces Coconut LaCroix
- 4 ounces of Pineapple juice
- Juice from 2 Limes
- 1/2 cup Citric acid
- 1 cup baking soda
- 1 cup Sugar
- 5g Gum acacia
- Water

INSTRUCTIONS:
- ☑ Measure all ingredients into a bowl.
- ☑ Work the mixture with your hands until it has a sandy texture.
- ☑ Form the mixture into balls and place it in a mold.
- ☑ Serve with 3 ounces of Coconut Vodka.

44. Fizzy Spicy Beer Bomb

MAKES: 4 bombs

INGREDIENTS:
- 1 1/2 teaspoons smoked paprika
- 1 teaspoon Worcestershire Sauce
- 3 tablespoons chili powder
- 1/2 teaspoon Mesquite Lime Sea Salt
- 2 teaspoons citric acid, food-grade
- 1 teaspoon Hot Sauce

INSTRUCTIONS:
- ☑ Combine the paprika, chili powder, lime sea salt, and citric acid in a mixing dish.
- ☑ Add a splash or two of Worcestershire sauce and hot sauce, then mix to combine.
- ☑ In a silicone mold, place 1 1/2 tablespoons to 2 tablespoons of the mixture. Firmly press down.
- ☑ Freeze the beer fizzy bombs for 4-6 hours, covered.
- ☑ Serve with a glass of beer.

45. Bellini Blush

MAKES: 10 bombs

INGREDIENTS:
- 5 ounces peach purée
- 1/2 cup Citric acid
- 5 ounces of simple syrup
- Water
- 1 cup baking soda
- 1 cup Sugar
- 5g Gum acacia

INSTRUCTIONS:
- ☑ Measure all ingredients into a bowl.
- ☑ Work the mixture with your hands until it has a sandy texture.
- ☑ Form the mixture into balls and place it in a mold.

46. <u>Lavender Lush bomb</u>

MAKES: 10 bombs

INGREDIENTS:
FOR GINGER AND LAVENDER SYRUP:
- 1 cup white sugar
- ½ cup water
- 4 ounces fresh ginger, scrubbed clean
- 2 teaspoons dried edible lavender, crushed

FOR LAVENDER LUSH BOMB:
- 1 cup baking soda
- 1 cup Sugar
- 1/2 cup Citric acid
- 5g Gum acacia

DIRECTIONS
FOR GINGER AND LAVENDER SYRUP:
- ☑ Place the ingredients for ginger and lavender syrup into a small pan and bring to a boil.
- ☑ Simmer for 10 minutes.
- ☑ Sieve and discard the ginger pulp.

FOR LAVENDER LUSH BOMB:
- ☑ Combine sugar, citric acid, and baking soda in a bowl.
- ☑ Add gum acacia and lavender syrup.
- ☑ Work the mixture with your hands until it has a sandy texture.
- ☑ Form the mixture into balls and place it in a mold.
- ☑ Serve the bomb in chilled vodka, iced tea, or water.

47. <u>Hangover Charcoal bomb</u>

MAKES: 10 bombs

INGREDIENTS:
- 6 ounces of fresh orange juice
- 1/4 cup maple syrup
- 6 ounces of fresh lemon juice
- Water
- 1 teaspoon Freshly grated ginger
- 1 teaspoon activated charcoal
- 1/2 cup Citric acid
- 1 cup baking soda
- 1 cup Sugar
- 5g Gum acacia

INSTRUCTIONS:
- ☑ Work everything together with your hands, until the mixture has turned into a sand consistency.
- ☑ Form the mixture into balls and place it in a mold.

48. Limoncello Fizzer

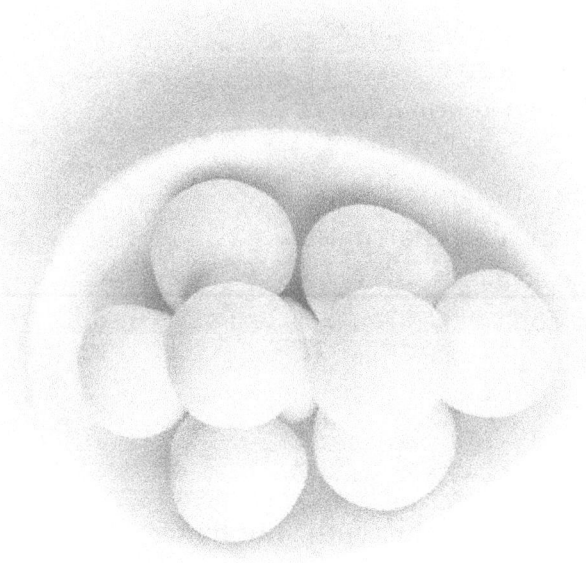

MAKES: 10 bombs

INGREDIENTS:
- 8 ounces of freshly-squeezed lemon juice
- 6 ounces oleo Saccharum (sugar-oil mixture)
- 1/2 cup Citric acid
- 1 cup baking soda
- 1 cup Sugar
- 5g Gum acacia
- Water

INSTRUCTIONS:
- ☑ Measure all ingredients into a bowl.
- ☑ Using enough water, combine with your hands until the mixture resembles sand.
- ☑ Form the mixture into balls and place it in a mold.
- ☑ This pairs well with gin or vodka.

49. **Old Fashioned**

MAKES: 10 bombs

INGREDIENTS:
- 2 ounces of barley tea
- 1/2 cup Water
- 1/2 cup Citric acid
- Juice of 1 orange
- 10 ounces Angostura bitters
- 1 cup baking soda
- 1 cup Sugar
- 5g Gum acacia
- Pinch Gold luster

DIRECTIONS
FOR THE TEA:
- ☑ Pour the water into a pitcher.
- ☑ Add the tea bag.
- ☑ Refrigerate for 2 hours then discard the tea bag.

FOR THE BOMB:
- ☑ Combine the dry ingredients in a bowl; Citric acid, baking soda, sugar, Gum acacia, and gold luster.
- ☑ Add the bitters, orange juice, and tea, then work the mixture with your hands until it resembles sand.
- ☑ Form the mixture into balls and place it in a mold.

50. Bubblegum Bomb

MAKES: 10 bombs

INGREDIENTS:
- For the Bubblegum Syrup:
- 2 cups water
- 1 cup granulated sugar
- 12 pieces bubblegum

FOR THE BOMB:
- 1/2 cup Citric acid
- 5g Gum acacia
- 1 cup baking soda

DIRECTIONS

FOR THE BUBBLEGUM SYRUP:
- ☑ In a medium saucepan, combine the sugar and water and bring to a boil.
- ☑ Reduce the heat to a simmer and stir in the bubblegum.
- ☑ Simmer for 10 minutes or until it starts to thicken.
- ☑ Remove from heat and strain syrup. Refrigerate to cool completely.

FOR THE BUBBLEGUM BOMB:
- ☑ Combine the dry ingredients in a bowl; Citric acid, baking soda, and Gum acacia.
- ☑ Add the Bubblegum Syrup and work the mixture with your hands.
- ☑ Form the mixture into balls and place it in a mold.

51. **Birthday Cake**

MAKES: 10 bombs

INGREDIENTS:
- 16 ounces vanilla cream soda
- Water
- 1/2 cup Citric acid
- ¼ cups Powdered Coffee Creamer
- 1 cup Powdered Sugar
- 1 cup baking soda
- 5g Gum acacia
- Pink food coloring
- Whipped cream and sprinkles for garnish

INSTRUCTIONS:
- ☑ Measure all ingredients, except the Whipped cream and sprinkles, into a bowl.
- ☑ Work the mixture with your hands until it has a sandy texture.
- ☑ Form the mixture into balls and place it in a mold.
- ☑ Decorate with whipped cream and sprinkles.

52. Bee's Knees

MAKES: 10 bombs

INGREDIENTS:
- 8 ounces of lemon juice, freshly squeezed
- 1/2 cup Citric acid
- 4 ounces honey
- 1 cup baking soda
- 1 cup Sugar
- 5g Gum acacia
- Water

INSTRUCTIONS:
- ☑ Measure all ingredients into a bowl.
- ☑ Work the mixture with your hands until it has a sandy texture.
- ☑ Form the mixture into balls and place it in a mold.

53. Berry Smash

MAKES: 10 bombs

INGREDIENTS:
- 4 ounces of freshly squeezed lime juice
- 4 ounces of stevia simple syrup
- 1/2 cup Citric acid
- 4 ounces of Raspberry syrup
- 4 ounces of Blackberry syrup
- 1 cup Sugar
- 1 cup baking soda
- 5g Gum acacia
- Water

INSTRUCTIONS:
- ☑ Measure all ingredients into a bowl.
- ☑ Work the mixture with your hands until it has a sandy texture.
- ☑ Form the mixture into balls and place it in a mold.
- ☑ Serve with Gin.

54. **Strawberry Basil Mojito**

MAKES: 10 bombs

INGREDIENTS:
- Juice of 1 lime
- 4 ounces of Mint syrup
- 1/2 cup Citric acid
- 4 ounces of Basil syrup
- 4 ounces of Strawberry syrup
- 1/4 cup stevia simple syrup
- 1 cup Sugar
- 1 cup baking soda
- 5g Gum acacia
- Water

INSTRUCTIONS:
- ☑ Measure all ingredients into a bowl.
- ☑ Work the mixture with your hands until it has a sandy texture.
- ☑ Form the mixture into balls and place it in a mold.
- ☑ Serve with Rum.

55. Grapefruit Crush

MAKES: 10 bombs

INGREDIENTS:
- 6 ounces of freshly squeezed lime juice
- 5g Gum acacia
- Water
- 3 ounces of stevia simple syrup
- 1 cup Sugar
- 1/2 cup Citric acid
- 6 ounces of freshly squeezed grapefruit juice
- 1 cup baking soda

INSTRUCTIONS:
- ☑ Measure all ingredients into a bowl.
- ☑ Work the mixture with your hands until it has a sandy texture.
- ☑ Form the mixture into balls and place it in a mold.
- ☑ Serve with Tequila.

56. Peaches n' Cream Bombs

MAKES: 6 bombs

INGREDIENTS:
PEACH SHELLS
- 1/2 cup red candy melts, melted
- 2 cups heavy cream
- 1 teaspoon vanilla
- 1/2 cup pink candy melts, melted
- 2 cups yellow candy melts, melted
- Whipped Cream
- 1/2 cup orange candy melts, melted
- 1 cup powdered sugar

FILLING
- 2 tablespoons butter
- 3 cups peaches, sliced
- 1 vanilla bean
- 1 chocolate pound cake, sliced

DIRECTIONS
PEACH SHELLS:
- ☑ Use red, orange, and pink candy melts to brush and dot the sides of 2-inch round silicone molds.
- ☑ After allowing for two minutes of setting, add the yellow candy melts to form a shell.
- ☑ Let the mixture partially firm before turning the molds over and pouring out the extra.
- ☑ Set in the refrigerator for approximately 10 minutes.

WHIPPED CREAM:
- ☑ Begin blending the heavy cream and sugar in the bowl of a stand mixer.
- ☑ Whip until firm peaks appear.
- ☑ Combine with vanilla.

FILLING
- ☑ Sauté the peaches and vanilla bean in butter in a skillet over medium heat until they start to soften.

- ☑ Let it cool and then spoon some peach filling into the chocolate shells, fill them two-thirds of the way with whipped cream, and then add a chocolate pound cake "pit" on top.
- ☑ Leave for 15 minutes to set in the freezer.
- ☑ Take the mold apart.
- ☑ Attach the two parts by pressing them together after piping a pink candy melt ring around the exterior.
- ☑ Set for 15 minutes.

57. Blueberry Bombs

MAKES: 6 bombs

INGREDIENTS:
BLUEBERRY GELEE:
- 1/4 cup water
- 1 1/2 cups blueberries
- 1/4-ounce packet of powdered gelatin
- 1 tablespoon honey
- 2 tablespoons sugar
- 2 teaspoons fresh lemon juice

BLUEBERRY SHELL
- 3 cups blue chocolate wafers, melted

WHIPPED CREAM
- 2 cups heavy cream
- 1 cup powdered sugar
- 1 teaspoon vanilla

DIRECTIONS
BLUEBERRY GELEE:
- ☑ Sprinkle the gelatin powder over the water, then leave for five minutes.
- ☑ Over medium heat, bring blueberries, honey, sugar, and lemon juice to a boil in a saucepan.
- ☑ Simmer until the sugar dissolves.
- ☑ Add the gelatin water and whisk for about 3 minutes, or until dissolved.
- ☑ Allow it to cool slightly before pouring it into silicone half-sphere molds.
- ☑ Chill for 1 hour.

BLUEBERRY SHELL:
- ☑ Fill the bottom and sides of two-inch silicone molds with blue chocolate wafers.
- ☑ Let it sit for a little while, then turn the molds upside down to pour out the extra.
- ☑ Set in the refrigerator for approximately 10 minutes.

WHIPPED CREAM:
- ☑ Combine the sugar and heavy cream.
- ☑ Fold in vanilla after whipping the cream until stiff peaks form.
- ☑ Place a little round of blueberry gelee on top of the whipped cream after filling the chocolate shells two-thirds of the way.
- ☑ Set in the freezer for an hour.
- ☑ Take the mold apart.
- ☑ Attach the two parts by pressing them together after piping a ring of blue chocolate around the exterior.
- ☑ Press lightly on the center top of the blueberry to form the top of the blueberry by dipping a tiny flower-shaped cookie cutter into some melted blue chocolate.
- ☑ Rest at room temperature for 15 minutes.

58. Cucumber Mint Twist

MAKES: 10 bombs

INGREDIENTS:
- 1/4 cup of freshly squeezed lemon juice
- 1/2 ounce stevia simple syrup
- Cucumber syrup
- Mint syrup
- 1 cup Sugar
- 1/2 cup Citric acid
- 1 cup baking soda
- 5g Gum acacia
- Water

INSTRUCTIONS:
- ☑ Measure all ingredients into a bowl.
- ☑ Work the mixture with your hands until it has a sandy texture.
- ☑ Form the mixture into balls and place it in a mold.
- ☑ Serve with Gin.

59. Cotton Candy Glitter Bombs

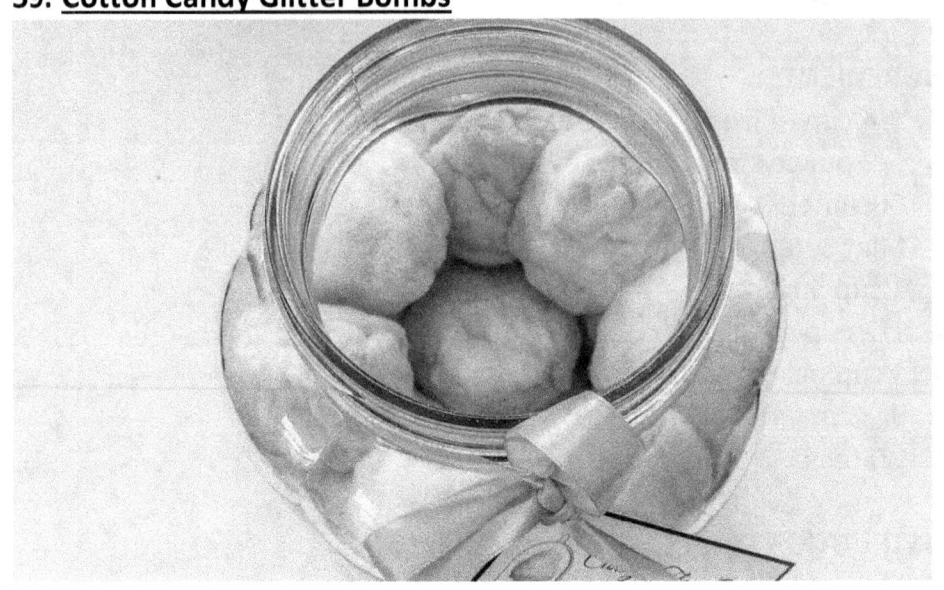

MAKES: 1 bomb

INGREDIENTS:
- Cotton Candy
- Edible Glitter or Luster Dust

INSTRUCTIONS:
- ☑ Take a handful of cotton candy and form an indentation in the center.
- ☑ Sprinkle some luster dust in the center.
- ☑ Roll the cotton candy into a ball, sealing the luster dust in the center.
- ☑ When ready to use, place it in a glass and top it with your favorite carbonated beverage, watching it dissolve.
- ☑ Stir it up and enjoy.

60. Koolaid Bombs

MAKES: 20 bombs

INGREDIENTS:
- 1/3 cups baking soda
- 1/4 cups cornstarch
- 1/2 cup powdered sugar
- 1/4 cup citric acid
- 1-2 packets of Kool-Aid
- 1-2 packets of pop rocks
- water
- sprinkles

INSTRUCTIONS:
- ☑ Combine baking soda, cornstarch, powdered sugar, citric acid, and Kool-Aid in a mixing bowl.
- ☑ Using your hands, mix in the water and dry the ingredients until the mixture resembles sand.
- ☑ Toss in a couple of packets of pop rocks and sprinkles.
- ☑ Roll the mixture into balls and place them in a mold.

61. Caramel Apple Cider Bombs

MAKES: 3 bombs

INGREDIENTS:
- Salted Caramel candy melts, melted
- A packet of Apple Cider drink mix

EQUIPMENT:
- XL Semi-sphere silicone mold

INSTRUCTIONS:
- ☑ Fill the silicone molds halfway with melted chocolate.
- ☑ Refrigerate or freeze for 10-15 minutes, or until they're easy to remove.
- ☑ Carefully remove the chocolate from the mold.
- ☑ Add apple cider drink mix to one chocolate half.
- ☑ In the microwave, heat a plate for around 15 seconds.
- ☑ Take the other chocolate half, split it in half, and set the open end on the hot plate for a few seconds to melt the chocolate.
- ☑ Connect the two halves of the chocolates and seal them together.
- ☑ Drizzle melted chocolate over the top and set aside to dry.
- ☑ Place the apple cider bomb in the bottom of a mug and top it with 6 ounces of boiling water.
- ☑ Stir well.

62. Candy floss bomb

MAKES: 10 bombs

INGREDIENTS:
- 800g sugar
- 240ml corn syrup
- 240ml water
- ¼ teaspoon salt
- 1 teaspoon raspberry extract
- 2 drops of food coloring
- Luster Dust

INSTRUCTIONS:
- ☑ Mix the sugar, corn syrup, water, and salt in a big, heavy pot over medium heat.
- ☑ Stir the sugar until it melts.
- ☑ Transfer the liquid to a heat-resistant container.
- ☑ Stir well after adding the extract and food coloring.
- ☑ Swing the whisk back and forth while holding it over the parchment so that little sugar strands fall onto the paper. Allow it to cool.
- ☑ Take a bunch of candy floss and sprinkle some luster dust in the center.
- ☑ Form a ball out of the candy, and press the luster dust into the center.

63. Azalea bomb

MAKES: 10 bombs

INGREDIENTS:
- 3/4 ounce lime juice
- 3/4 ounce pineapple juice
- 4 dashes grenadine
- 1/2 cup Citric acid
- 1 cup baking soda
- 5g Gum acacia
- Water

INSTRUCTIONS:
- ☑ Measure all ingredients into a bowl.
- ☑ Work the mixture with your hands until it has a sandy texture.
- ☑ Form the mixture into balls and place it in a mold.

64. Mango batida bomb

MAKES: 10 bombs

INGREDIENTS:
- 1/4 cup orange juice
- 2 1/4 ounces of mango juice
- 1/2 cup Citric acid
- 1 cup baking soda
- 1 cup Sugar
- 5g Gum acacia
- Pinch Gold luster
- Water

INSTRUCTIONS:
- ☑ Measure all ingredients into a bowl.
- ☑ Work the mixture with your hands until it has a sandy texture.
- ☑ Form mixture into balls and place in a mold to set.
- ☑ Unmold, then store in the refrigerator or on the counter in an airtight container.

65. Frosted cranberry bomb

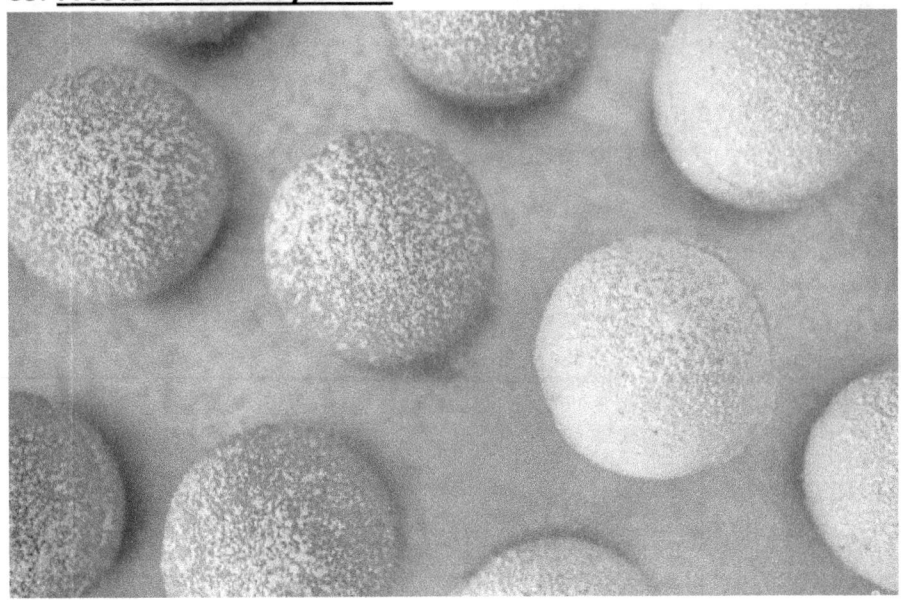

MAKES: 10 bombs

INGREDIENTS:
- 3/4 cup Cranberry Juice
- Sugared Cranberries, muddled
- Water
- 1/2 cup Citric acid
- 1 cup baking soda
- 1 cup Sugar
- 5g Gum acacia
- Pinch Gold luster

INSTRUCTIONS:
- ☑ Measure all ingredients into a bowl.
- ☑ Work the mixture with your hands until it has a sandy texture.
- ☑ Form mixture into balls and place in a mold to set.
- ☑ Unmold, then store in the refrigerator or on the counter in an airtight container.

66. Blue raspberry bomb

MAKES: 10 bombs

INGREDIENTS:
- 2 ounces lemonade powder
- Water
- 2 ounces of raspberry syrup
- 1/2 cup Citric acid
- 1 cup baking soda
- 1 cup Sugar
- 5g Gum acacia
- Pinch Gold luster

INSTRUCTIONS:
- ☑ In a large punch bowl, stir together lemonade powder and water until lemonade powder dissolves. Add the other ingredients.
- ☑ Work the mixture with your hands until it has a sandy texture.
- ☑ Make the mixture into balls and put them into a mold to set.
- ☑ Unmold, then store in the refrigerator or on the counter in an airtight container.

67. <u>Raspberry orange bomb</u>

MAKES: 10 bombs

INGREDIENTS:
- 1/4 cup raspberry syrup
- Juice of 1 lime
- Juice of 1 medium orange
- 1/2 cup Citric acid
- 1 cup baking soda
- Water
- 1 cup Sugar
- 5g Gum acacia

INSTRUCTIONS:
- ☑ Measure all ingredients into a bowl.
- ☑ Work the mixture with your hands until it has a sandy texture.
- ☑ Form mixture into balls and place in a mold to set.
- ☑ Unmold, then store in the refrigerator or on the counter in an airtight container.

68. Lemon drop bomb

MAKES: 10 bombs

INGREDIENTS:
FOR THE LEMON SUGAR
- Zest from 1 lemon
- 1/2 cup granulated sugar

FOR THE BOMB
- 1 ½ tablespoons simple syrup
- Water
- 1 cup baking soda
- Juice from 1/2 large lemon
- 1 cup Sugar
- 1/2 cup Citric acid
- 5g Gum acacia

INSTRUCTIONS:
- ☑ Add sugar to a plate and, using your fingers, rub the zest into the sugar until it is fragrant and yellow.
- ☑ Add all ingredients to a bowl.
- ☑ Work the mixture with your hands until it has a sandy texture.
- ☑ Form mixture into balls and place in a mold to set.
- ☑ Unmold, then store in the refrigerator or on the counter in an airtight container.

69. Cosmo Bomb

MAKES: 10 bombs

INGREDIENTS:
- 10 ml Reduced Sugar Cranberry Juice
- 1/2 cup Citric acid
- 5 ml orange juice
- Water
- 5 ml freshly squeezed lime juice
- 1 cup baking soda
- 1 cup Sugar
- 5g Gum acacia

INSTRUCTIONS:
- ☑ Measure all ingredients into a bowl.
- ☑ Work the mixture with your hands until it has a sandy texture.
- ☑ Form mixture into balls and place in a mold to set.
- ☑ Unmold, then store in the refrigerator or on the counter in an airtight container.

70. Peacharita Bomb

MAKES: 10 bombs

INGREDIENTS:
- ½ ounce agave syrup
- 1-2 ounces of fresh Peach Purée
- Water
- 1 cup baking soda
- ¾ ounce freshly squeezed lime juice
- 5g Gum acacia
- 1/2 cup Citric acid
- 1 cup Sugar

INSTRUCTIONS:
- ☑ Measure all ingredients into a bowl.
- ☑ Work the mixture with your hands until it has a sandy texture.
- ☑ Form mixture into balls and place in a mold to set.
- ☑ Unmold, then store in the refrigerator or on the counter in an airtight container.

71. Passion Hurricane bomb

MAKES: 10 bombs

INGREDIENTS:
- 2 cups of passion fruit juice
- Water
- 3/4 cup of lime juice
- 3 tablespoons of grenadine
- 1/2 cup Citric acid
- 1 cup plus 2 tablespoons of sugar
- 1 cup baking soda
- 5g Gum acacia

INSTRUCTIONS:
- ☑ Measure all ingredients into a bowl.
- ☑ Work the mixture with your hands until it has a sandy texture.
- ☑ Form mixture into balls and place in a mold to set.
- ☑ Unmold, then store in the refrigerator or on the counter in an airtight container.

72. Michelada Bomb

MAKES: 10 bombs

INGREDIENTS:
- 6 dashes of hot sauce
- 3 dashes of soy sauce
- 1-3 dashes of Worcestershire sauce
- ¼-⅓ cup of lime juice
- 1/2 cup Citric acid
- 1 cup baking soda
- 1 cup Sugar
- 5g Gum acacia

INSTRUCTIONS:
- ☑ Measure all ingredients into a bowl.
- ☑ Work the mixture with your hands until it has a sandy texture.
- ☑ Form mixture into balls and place in a mold to set.
- ☑ Unmold, then store in the refrigerator or on the counter in an airtight container.

73. Zombie Cocktail bomb

MAKES: 10 bombs

INGREDIENTS:
- 1/2 cup Citric acid
- 2 ounces of papaya juice
- 2 ounces of lime juice
- Water
- 2 ounces of pineapple juice
- 1 cup baking soda
- 1 cup Superfine sugar
- 5g Gum acacia

INSTRUCTIONS:
- ☑ Measure all ingredients into a bowl.
- ☑ Work the mixture with your hands until it has a sandy texture.
- ☑ Form mixture into balls and place in a mold to set.
- ☑ Unmold, then store in the refrigerator or on the counter in an airtight container.

74. Sazerac Bomb

MAKES: 10 bombs

INGREDIENTS:
- 2 dashes of Angostura bitters
- 3 dashes of Peychaud's bitters
- 1/2 cup Citric acid
- 5g Gum acacia
- 1 cup baking soda
- Water
- 1 cup Superfine sugar

INSTRUCTIONS:
- ☑ Measure all ingredients into a bowl.
- ☑ Work the mixture with your hands until it has a sandy texture.
- ☑ Form mixture into balls and place in a mold to set.
- ☑ Unmold, then store in the refrigerator or on the counter in an airtight container.

75. Mango Mule

MAKES: 10 bombs

INGREDIENTS:
- 6 ounces of cucumber syrup
- 4 ounces of honey syrup
- 1.5 ounces mango purée
- 1.5 ounces of fresh lime juice
- Water
- 1/2 cup Citric acid
- 1 cup baking soda
- 1 cup Superfine sugar
- 5g Gum acacia

INSTRUCTIONS:
- ☑ Muddle cucumber and honey syrup.
- ☑ Add the mango purée and lime juice and mix vigorously.
- ☑ Add all other ingredients.
- ☑ Work the mixture with your hands until it has a sandy texture.
- ☑ Form mixture into balls and place in a mold to set.
- ☑ Unmold, then store in the refrigerator or on the counter in an airtight container.

76. Citrus Fizz

MAKES: 10 bombs

INGREDIENTS:
- 1.75 ounces Seedlip Grove 42
- 0.75 ounces organic marmalade cordial
- Water
- 1/2 cup Citric acid
- 1 cup baking soda
- 1 cup Superfine sugar
- 5g Gum acacia

INSTRUCTIONS:
- ☑ Measure all ingredients into a bowl.
- ☑ Work the mixture with your hands until it has a sandy texture.
- ☑ Form mixture into balls and place in a mold to set.
- ☑ Unmold, then store in the refrigerator or on the counter in an airtight container.

77. Virgin Cucumber Bomb

MAKES: 10 bombs

INGREDIENTS:
- 4 ounces of cucumber syrup
- 1 cup baking soda
- 4 ounces of simple syrup
- 1/2 cup Citric acid
- 1 cup Superfine sugar
- 4 ounces of fresh lime juice
- Water
- 5g Gum acacia

INSTRUCTIONS:
- ☑ Measure all ingredients into a bowl.
- ☑ Work the mixture with your hands until it has a sandy texture.
- ☑ Form mixture into balls and place in a mold to set.
- ☑ Unmold, then store in the refrigerator or on the counter in an airtight container.

78. Ritual apple bomb

MAKES: 10 bombs

INGREDIENTS:
- 2 ounces of apple cider or apple juice
- 1/2 cup Citric acid
- 2 dashes bitters
- Water
- Pinch Cinnamon powder
- 1 cup baking soda
- 1 cup Superfine sugar
- 5g Gum acacia

INSTRUCTIONS:
- ☑ Measure all ingredients into a bowl.
- ☑ Work the mixture with your hands until it has a sandy texture.
- ☑ Form mixture into balls and place in a mold to set.
- ☑ Unmold, then store in the refrigerator or on the counter in an airtight container.

79. **Shirley Ginger**

MAKES: 10 bombs

INGREDIENTS:
- 0.25 cup grenadine
- Water
- 3 Tablespoons lime juice
- 1 cup baking soda
- 3 Tablespoons Ginger syrup
- 5g Gum acacia
- 1/2 cup Citric acid
- 1 cup Superfine sugar

INSTRUCTIONS:
- ☑ Measure all ingredients into a bowl.
- ☑ Work the mixture with your hands until it has a sandy texture.
- ☑ Form mixture into balls and place in a mold to set.
- ☑ Unmold, then store in the refrigerator or on the counter in an airtight container.
- ☑ Enjoy with a glass of Lemon Lime Ginger Beer.

80. Watermelon Margarita

MAKES: 10 bombs

INGREDIENTS:
- 0.5 cup watermelon juice
- 0.5 cups fresh lime juice
- 4 teaspoon agave
- Water
- 1/2 cup Citric acid
- 1 cup baking soda
- 1 cup Superfine sugar
- 5g Gum acacia

INSTRUCTIONS:
- ☑ Measure all ingredients into a bowl.
- ☑ Work the mixture with your hands until it has a sandy texture.
- ☑ Form mixture into balls and place in a mold to set.
- ☑ Unmold, then store in the refrigerator or on the counter in an airtight container.

81. Berry Burlesque

MAKES: 10 bombs

INGREDIENTS:
- 4 ounces of lime juice
- 4 ounces of honey syrup
- 4 ounces of mint syrup
- 2 ounces black currant purée
- Water
- 1/2 cup Citric acid
- 1 cup baking soda
- 1 cup Superfine sugar
- 5g Gum acacia

INSTRUCTIONS:
- ☑ Measure all ingredients into a bowl.
- ☑ Work the mixture with your hands until it has a sandy texture.
- ☑ Form mixture into balls and place in a mold to set.
- ☑ Unmold, then store in the refrigerator or on the counter in an airtight container.
- ☑ Enjoy Ginger Beer

82. Lavender Lemonade

MAKES: 10 bombs

INGREDIENTS:
- 6 cups water
- 0.5 cup honey
- 5 Tablespoons dried lavender
- 1 cup fresh lemon juice, strained
- 1/2 cup Citric acid
- 1 cup baking soda
- 1 cup Superfine sugar
- 5g Gum acacia

INSTRUCTIONS:
- ☑ Measure all ingredients into a bowl.
- ☑ Work the mixture with your hands until it has a sandy texture.
- ☑ Form mixture into balls and place in a mold to set.
- ☑ Unmold, then store in the refrigerator or on the counter in an airtight container.

83. Rosemary Blueberry Smash

MAKES: 10 bombs

INGREDIENTS:
- 6 ounces of Blueberry syrup
- 4 ounces of honey syrup
- 4 ounces fresh lemon juice, strained
- Water
- Pinch dried rosemary
- 1/2 cup Citric acid
- 1 cup baking soda
- 1 cup Superfine sugar
- 5g Gum acacia

INSTRUCTIONS:
- ☑ Measure all ingredients into a bowl.
- ☑ Work the mixture with your hands until it has a sandy texture.
- ☑ Form mixture into balls and place in a mold to set.
- ☑ Unmold, then store in the refrigerator or on the counter in an airtight container.

84. Coconut, Cucumber & Mint Bomb

MAKES: 10 bombs

INGREDIENTS:
- 3 ounces of coconut water
- 3 ounces of cucumber syrup
- 3 ounces of mint syrup
- 0.5 cup of lime juice
- Water
- 1/2 cup Citric acid
- 1 cup baking soda
- 1 cup Superfine sugar
- 5g Gum acacia

INSTRUCTIONS:
- ☑ Measure all ingredients into a bowl.
- ☑ Work the mixture with your hands until it has a sandy texture.
- ☑ Form mixture into balls and place in a mold to set.
- ☑ Unmold, then store in the refrigerator or on the counter in an airtight container.

85. <u>Watermelon & Mint bomb</u>

MAKES: 10 bombs

INGREDIENTS:
- Water
- 1 Tablespoon watermelon syrup
- 1 Tablespoon lime juice
- 1 Tablespoon mint syrup
- 1 Tablespoon jalapeño syrup
- 1/2 cup Citric acid
- 1 cup baking soda
- 1 cup Superfine sugar
- 5g Gum acacia

INSTRUCTIONS:
- ☑ Measure all ingredients into a bowl.
- ☑ Work the mixture with your hands until it has a sandy texture.
- ☑ Form mixture into balls and place in a mold to set.
- ☑ Unmold, then store in the refrigerator or on the counter in an airtight container.

86. **Lemongrass & Jasmine bomb**

MAKES: 10 bombs

INGREDIENTS:
- 1/4 cup lemon grass syrup
- 1/4 cup simple syrup
- 1/4 cup lemon
- 4 ounces of jasmine tea
- 2 ounces lychee juice
- Water
- 1/2 cup Citric acid
- 1 cup baking soda
- 1 cup Superfine sugar
- 5g Gum acacia

INSTRUCTIONS:
- ☑ Measure all ingredients into a bowl.
- ☑ Work the mixture with your hands until it has a sandy texture.
- ☑ Form mixture into balls and place in a mold to set.
- ☑ Unmold, then store in the refrigerator or on the counter in an airtight container.

87. **Blueberry Mojito**

MAKES: 10 bombs

INGREDIENTS:
- 2 ounces of mint syrup
- 2 ounces of blueberry syrup
- 2 ounces of lime juice
- 2 ounces of simple syrup
- Water
- 1/2 cup Citric acid
- 1 cup baking soda
- 1 cup Superfine sugar
- 5g Gum acacia

INSTRUCTIONS:
- ☑ Measure all ingredients into a bowl.
- ☑ Work the mixture with your hands until it has a sandy texture.
- ☑ Form mixture into balls and place in a mold to set.
- ☑ Unmold, then store in the refrigerator or on the counter in an airtight container.

88. Virgin Paloma

MAKES: 10 bombs

INGREDIENTS:
- 3 ounces of lime juice
- 3 ounces grapefruit juice
- 3 ounces agave syrup
- Water
- Healthy pinch of sea salt
- 1/2 cup Citric acid
- 1 cup baking soda
- 1 cup Superfine sugar
- 5g Gum acacia

INSTRUCTIONS:
- ☑ Measure all ingredients into a bowl.
- ☑ Work the mixture with your hands until it has a sandy texture.
- ☑ Form mixture into balls and place in a mold to set.
- ☑ Unmold, then store in the refrigerator or on the counter in an airtight container.

89. Wildcat Cooler

MAKES: 10 bombs

INGREDIENTS:
- 1 cup blueberry syrup
- Water
- 1 cup sugar
- 1 lemon, juiced
- 1/2 cup Citric acid
- 1 cup baking soda
- 5g Gum acacia
- Pinch Gold luster

INSTRUCTIONS:
- ☑ In a big saucepan, combine the blueberries, sugar, and water. Bring to a boil.
- ☑ For 15 minutes, simmer on a lower heat.
- ☑ Use a fine sieve to separate the juice's particles from the juice, and then set the solids aside.
- ☑ Combine the dry ingredients in a bowl, including the gum acacia, baking soda, sugar, and citric acid.
- ☑ Add the blueberry mixture and mash the ingredients together with your fingertips until they resemble sand.
- ☑ Form the mixture into balls and put them in a mold.

90. Pineapple Ginger Beer Bomb

MAKES: 10 bombs

INGREDIENTS:
- Water
- 1 cup baking soda
- 4 ounces of pineapple juice
- 4 ounces of ginger syrup
- 4 ounces of freshly squeezed lime juice
- 1/2 cup Citric acid
- 1 cup Superfine sugar
- 5g Gum acacia

INSTRUCTIONS:
- ☑ Measure all ingredients into a bowl.
- ☑ Work the mixture with your hands until it has a sandy texture.
- ☑ Form mixture into balls and place in a mold to set.
- ☑ Unmold, then store in the refrigerator or on the counter in an airtight container.

91. Seedlip Spice & Tonic

MAKES: 10 bombs

INGREDIENTS:
- 2 ounces Seedlip Spice 94
- Tonic syrup to taste
- Water
- Pinch Star anise powder
- Pinch Cinnamon powder
- 1/2 cup Citric acid
- 1 cup baking soda
- 1 cup Superfine sugar
- 5g Gum acacia

INSTRUCTIONS:
- ☑ Measure all ingredients into a bowl.
- ☑ Work the mixture with your hands until it has a sandy texture.
- ☑ Form mixture into balls and place in a mold to set.
- ☑ Unmold, then store in the refrigerator or on the counter in an airtight container.

92. Pineapple Cobbler

MAKES: 10 bombs

INGREDIENTS:
- 4 ounces of strawberry juice
- 6 ounces of pineapple juice
- 1/2 cup Citric acid
- 2 ounces of lime juice
- 1 cup baking soda
- 1 cup Superfine sugar
- Water
- 5g Gum acacia

INSTRUCTIONS:
- ☑ Measure all ingredients into a bowl.
- ☑ Work the mixture with your hands until it has a sandy texture.
- ☑ Form mixture into balls and place in a mold to set.
- ☑ Unmold, then store in the refrigerator or on the counter in an airtight container.

93. Tahitian Coffee

MAKES: 10 bombs

INGREDIENTS:
- 2 ounces of lime juice
- 1 cup baking soda
- 1/4 cup simple syrup
- 1/4 cup passion fruit purée
- 2 ounces cold brew concentrate
- 3 ounces honey syrup
- Water
- 2 ounces guava purée
- 1/2 cup Citric acid
- 2 ounces of orange juice
- 1 cup Superfine sugar
- 5g Gum acacia

INSTRUCTIONS:
- ☑ Measure all ingredients into a bowl.
- ☑ Work the mixture with your hands until it has a sandy texture.
- ☑ Form mixture into balls and place in a mold to set.
- ☑ Unmold, then store in the refrigerator or on the counter in an airtight container.

94. Raspberry Bee's Knees

MAKES: 10 bombs

INGREDIENTS:
- Filtered water
- 4 ounces lemon
- 4 ounces honey
- 1/2 cup Citric acid
- 4 ounces of raspberry syrup
- 1 cup baking soda
- 1 cup Superfine sugar
- 5g Gum acacia

INSTRUCTIONS:
- ☑ Measure all ingredients into a bowl.
- ☑ Work the mixture with your hands until it has a sandy texture.
- ☑ Form mixture into balls and place in a mold to set.
- ☑ Unmold, then store in the refrigerator or on the counter in an airtight container.

95. Pina Serrano Margarita

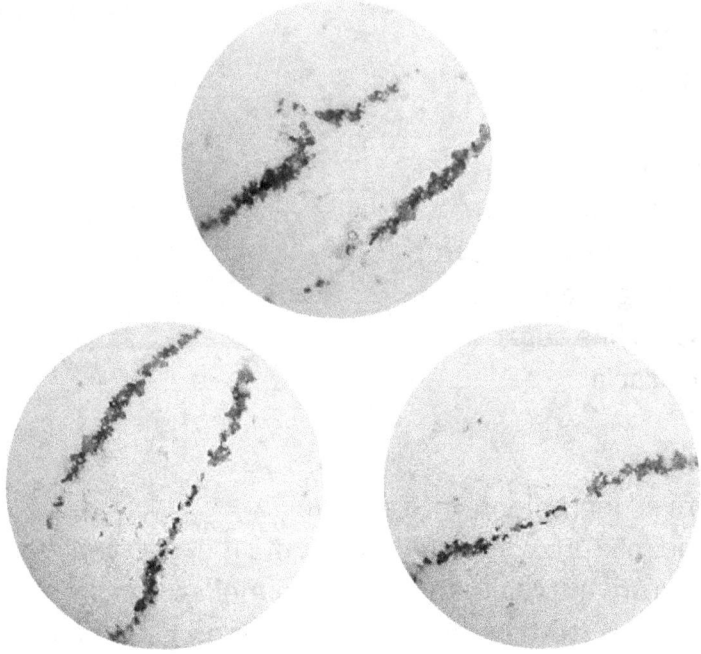

MAKES: 10 bombs

INGREDIENTS:
- 6 ounces of pineapple juice
- 3 ounces of lime juice
- Water
- 3 ounces of simple syrup
- Pinch Serrano chile powder
- 1 cup baking soda
- 1 cup Superfine sugar
- 1/2 cup Citric acid
- 5g Gum acacia

INSTRUCTIONS:
- ☑ Measure all ingredients into a bowl.
- ☑ Work the mixture with your hands until it has a sandy texture.
- ☑ Form mixture into balls and place in a mold to set.
- ☑ Unmold, then store in the refrigerator or on the counter in an airtight container.

96. Nopaloma bomb

MAKES: 10 bombs

INGREDIENTS:
- 6 ounces of freshly squeezed grapefruit juice
- 1/2 cup Citric acid
- 4 ounces of freshly squeezed lime juice
- 3 ounces of agave nectar
- Water
- Pinch Salt
- 1 cup baking soda
- 1 cup Superfine sugar
- 5g Gum acacia

INSTRUCTIONS:
- ☑ Measure all ingredients into a bowl.
- ☑ Work the mixture with your hands until it has a sandy texture.
- ☑ Form mixture into balls and place in a mold to set.
- ☑ Unmold, then store in the refrigerator or on the counter in an airtight container.

97. Revitalizer Bomb

MAKES: 10 bombs

INGREDIENTS:
- 5 ounces carrot juice
- Water
- 5g Gum acacia
- 1 cup baking soda
- 8 ounces of apple juice
- 1/4 cup ginger syrup
- 1/4 cup lime juice
- 1/2 cup Citric acid
- 1 cup Superfine sugar

INSTRUCTIONS:
- ☑ Measure all ingredients into a bowl.
- ☑ Work the mixture with your hands until it has a sandy texture.
- ☑ Form mixture into balls and place in a mold to set.
- ☑ Unmold, then store in the refrigerator or on the counter in an airtight container.

98. Arnold Palmer's Fizzy Bomb

Makes: 10 Bombs

INGREDIENTS:
- ½ cup ultrafine pure cane sugar
- ½ cup powdered sugar
- 2 teaspoon baking soda
- 1 ½ teaspoon sweat tea liquid water enhancer
- 1 ½ teaspoon lemonade liquid water enhancer
- 6 ounces of lemon sparkling water
- Add Lemon slices, for garnish
- Lemon slices, for garnish

EQUIPMENT
- 2 small bowls
- 2 (1 teaspoon) measures
- Rimmed tray
- Ice
- 12-ounces glass

INSTRUCTIONS:
- ☑ Combine ultrafine sugar, powdered sugar, and baking soda in a small bowl. Place 2/3 cup mixture into a bowl; mix in sweet tea liquid water enhancer. In the remaining 1/3 cup mixture, stir in the lemonade water enhancer. Both mixtures should resemble wet sand.
- ☑ Press the mixture alternatively into 2 (1 teaspoon) rounded measuring spoons, leaving some excess at top of the spoons. Invert one spoon on top of the other. Press spoons together and shake lightly.
- ☑ Remove one spoon and invert the bomb into your hand. Remove the remaining spoon and place the bomb on a rimmed tray. Repeat with the remaining mixture. Let dry for 4 hours before serving. Store covered at room temperature for up to 2 days.
- ☑ To serve, combine lemon sparkling water in a 12-ounces glass. Add 1 dried bomb; stir to mix well. Add crushed ice to the glass.

99. Prosecco Rose

MAKES: 10 bombs

INGREDIENTS:
- 8 ounces rose water
- 8 ounces elderflower water
- 1 cup baking soda
- Pinch organic Bulgarian rosebuds
- Pinch edible 24K gold dust
- 1/2 cup Citric acid
- 1 cup Sugar
- 5g Gum acacia
- Water

INSTRUCTIONS:
- ☑ Measure all ingredients into a bowl.
- ☑ Work the mixture with your hands until it has a sandy texture.
- ☑ Form the mixture into balls and place it in a mold.
- ☑ Goes well with sparkling wine or Prosecco with a splash of sparking soda.

100. **Fruity Drink Bombs**

MAKES: 6 bombs

INGREDIENTS:
- 1 small can fruit cocktail, diced
- 2 grams of powdered agar
- 1 tablespoon sugar
- 2 teaspoons lemon juice
- 250ml Water and fruit syrup
- Strawberries, finely diced
- Kiwi, finely diced
- Blueberries, finely diced

INSTRUCTIONS:
- ☑ In a saucepan, combine the powdered agar, sugar, lemon juice, water, and syrup mixture.
- ☑ Bring to a boil.
- ☑ Simmer for 2 minutes.
- ☑ Pour into round ice cube molds.
- ☑ Drop pieces of fruit into molds and pour the agar mixture on top.
- ☑ Snap the mold cover in place and refrigerate for about 1 hour.
- ☑ Place fruit bombs into individual glasses and serve with sparkling wine.

CONCLUSION

We hope you enjoyed this collection of hot chocolate bombs recipes and that they have brought a little bit of joy and warmth into your life. Hot chocolate bombs are not only delicious but also fun to make and share with others, and we hope that you will enjoy making them as much as we did.

Whether you prefer classic milk chocolate, or more unique flavors like peppermint, salted caramel, or red velvet, there is a recipe in this cookbook for everyone. We have included step-by-step instructions and helpful tips to ensure that your hot chocolate bombs turn out perfectly every time.

Thank you for choosing the Hot Chocolate Bombs Cookbook, and we hope that these recipes will become a staple in your kitchen during the cold winter months or any time you need a little pick-me-up. Don't forget to share your creations with us on social media using #hotchocolatebombs!

www.ingramcontent.com/pod-product-compliance
Lightning Source LLC
LaVergne TN
LVHW021710060526
838200LV00050B/2590